Contents

YORK HANDBOOKS

GENERAL EDITOR:
Professor A.N. Jeffares
(*University of Stirling*)

STUDYING CHAUCER

Elisabeth Brewer

MA (BIRMINGHAM)
*Senior Lecturer in English,
Homerton College of Education, Cambridge*

LONGMAN
YORK PRESS

YORK PRESS
Immeuble Esseily, Place Riad Solh, Beirut.

LONGMAN GROUP LIMITED
Longman House,
Burnt Mill,
Harlow,
Essex.

First published 1984
ISBN 0 582 79275 4
Printed in Hong Kong by
Wilture Printing Co Ltd.

Preface

This Handbook is intended primarily for students who are unfamiliar with medieval writers and their background. In it, I have tried to indicate what the modern reader needs to know in order to enjoy and begin to understand Chaucer. We can still, even today, six hundred years later, find much that is familiar and fundamentally true to human experience in Chaucer's poems, and recognise our kinship with the medieval men and women of whom and for whom he wrote. Yet there are inevitably patterns of thought that are strange to us, social and religious attitudes that are unfamiliar, and literary conventions that are different from those to which we are now accustomed.

I have endeavoured, as far as possible in the space available, to show what Chaucer's poems are 'about'; as well as what is of lasting significance in his work, and how we can evaluate it as literature. I have not attempted to include the more detailed, technical information which does contribute to the deeper understanding of the poems, but which is readily available elsewhere. The Bibliography will guide the reader to more scholarly, advanced, and technical studies, as they are required, and so to a more extensive knowledge of medieval literature and life.

All references to Chaucer's writings are to *The Works of Geoffrey Chaucer*, edited by F. N. Robinson, Oxford University Press, 2nd edition, 1957.

CHRONOLOGY

	Chaucer's life	*Historical events*
1337		Declaration of war with France (the Hundred Years' War)
*c.*1340–5	Chaucer born	
1348–9		The Black Death
1348–58		Boccaccio writing his collection of tales, the *Decameron*
1357	Chaucer becomes a page in the household of the Countess of Ulster	
1359–60	Chaucer on military service captured and ransomed	
1366	Journey to Spain	
*c.*1366	Chaucer married to Philippa Roet	
1367	Appointed Yeoman in the King's Household	
1369	Campaign in France *The Book of the Duchess* Appointed Esquire of the King's Household	Deaths of Queen Philippa and Blanche, Duchess of Lancaster
1372–3	First journey to Italy	
1374	Appointed Comptroller of Customs. *The House of Fame* begun	Death of Petrarch
1375		Death of Boccaccio
1376–7	Journeys abroad on the King's secret affairs	(1377) Death of Edward III, accession of Richard II
1378	Second Italian journey, to Lombardy	
1381		The Peasants' Revolt
*c.*1380–2	*The Parliament of Fowls*	
1382–5	Translation of Boethius' *Consolation of Philosophy*; *Troilus and Criseyde*; *Anelida and Arcite*	
1385	Chaucer appoints a permanent deputy for Comptrollership J.P. in Kent	
1385–6	*The Legend of Good Women*	
1386	Knight of the Shire for Kent. Later loses Comptrollership	
1387–1400	*The Canterbury Tales*	
1389	Clerk to the King's Works	
1391	Gives up Clerkship; appointed Subforester	
1394	Extra grant for good service	Death of Queen Anne
1399	Grants confirmed by Henry IV	Deposition of Richard II, succeeded by Henry IV
1400	25 October: Chaucer's death	Death of Richard II

Part 1

Chaucer and his world

Chaucer's life

Geoffrey Chaucer was born, probably in London, some time between 1340 and 1345. He was the son of a prosperous wine-merchant, connected with the royal court. Edward III was on the throne, and in 1337 had asserted his claim to extensive territories in France in the Hundred Years' War. When Chaucer was still a small boy, bubonic plague came to England: the virulent outbreak of 1348–9, known as the Black Death, killed off a high proportion of the population. He was lucky to survive the epidemic, as well as the subsequent recurrences of plague later in the century. The fourteenth century was, not surprisingly, an age of unusual tension, but it was also an age of great cultural achievement. For the fortunate survivors of the Black Death, the depopulation of the countryside meant that more food was available, and wages rose; but the war with France had to be financed, and high taxation caused much unrest. Chaucer lived through the Peasants' Revolt of 1381, and the deposition and murder of Richard II, to whose court he was attached, by Henry IV. Of the troubles of the time, Chaucer has little to say in his writing; but his work testifies to the positive achievements of an age in which learning and commerce, art and architecture and music and poetry flourished.

Nothing is known of Chaucer's childhood or early education. We first hear of him as a page in the household of the Countess of Ulster. The Countess was the wife of Prince Lionel, the second son of Edward III, so Chaucer was introduced early into courtly circles. At this stage in his life, he would have been given the social training considered appropriate for a young man at court, as well as some training in the military arts of the day.

Two years later he himself took part in the war in France and was captured, but soon ransomed. After this, nothing is known for certain of his life for some years, but he may well have gone to study at the Inner Temple in London, where he would have continued his general education in preparation for a professional and diplomatic career. In 1366 he travelled to Spain on some sort of official business, and also at about this time was married to Philippa Roet, who had been a member of the household of the Countess of Ulster when he was a young page. She was a 'damoiselle' of Queen Philippa in 1366, while her sister was later to become first the mistress and eventually the third wife of John of Gaunt, Duke of Lancaster, the most powerful nobleman in the kingdom. Chaucer therefore always had courtly connections.

In 1369 he was in France again, this time with John of Gaunt. Meanwhile, Blanche, Gaunt's first wife, died of plague and Chaucer soon after wrote *The Book of the Duchess* as an elegy for her. His wife Philippa later became lady-in-waiting to Gaunt's second wife, Constance of Castille, and both she and Chaucer were given annuities as reward for their services.

Chaucer had been made a Yeoman in the King's household in 1367, and from this time on he made frequent journeys abroad in the service of the king. He was in Italy in the winter of 1372–3, and went to Florence, but nothing is known for certain as to what he did and whom he met, though his great contemporaries, Petrarch and Boccaccio, were still alive. He had a working knowledge of Italian – though we do not know when or how he acquired it – but his command of this language was never equal to his command of French.

In 1374 Chaucer became Comptroller of Customs, a post which required some expertise in accounting, though it carried with it less power and responsibility than the term Comptroller itself suggests. He was to hold the post for the next twelve and a half years, during which time he also managed to produce a number of major works, and to make further journeys abroad on official business. It was during this period of his life that he wrote *The House of Fame*, as well as *The Parliament of Fowls*; he also translated a Latin work by Boethius, *The Consolation of Philosophy*, entitled *Boece*, and completed one of his greatest works, *Troilus and Criseyde. Anelida and Arcite*, and unfinished fragment, also dates from this time.

In 1385 Chaucer got a deputy for his work as Comptroller of Customs, became a Justice of the Peace for Kent, and next year was elected Knight of the Shire for Kent and gave up his work at the Customs House. He probably hoped to have more time for writing: by 1387, he seems to have begun work on *The Canterbury Tales*. Two years later, however, Richard II (who as a young boy had succeeded Edward III in 1377) made him Clerk of the King's Works. It was a demanding job which he relinquished after two years, to become a Sub-forester. From this time on he continued to receive financial rewards from the king; and when in 1399 John of Gaunt's son Henry deposed and supplanted Richard II, Chaucer's grants from Richard were confirmed by his successor. He took a house in the garden of Westminster Abbey, but before the end of 1400 he was dead.

Chaucer's busy life brought him into contact with people in many different walks of life, at court, at home and abroad, and in the war with France. As Comptroller and as Knight of the Shire for Kent, as well as in his other public offices, he was involved in the world of affairs, yet all his life he managed to read widely, as well as to achieve an immense poetic output. He must have been an unassuming man, who played a modest part at the centre of things with tact and discretion.

Courtly life

Throughout much of his life, Chaucer was attached to the royal court, first that of Edward III and then later, the court of Richard II. This, however, did not prevent him from having very wide experience of life in general, for his connection with the court brought with it involvement in several aspects of government.

In the fourteenth century, the royal court was not simply a social institution. It was also the means by which the country was governed, and many of those within its orbit were actively concerned with the affairs of the country in different capacities. In the earlier part of the century the court had moved about the country, as the king moved from one castle or palace to another. Such a large body of people would naturally exhaust the resources of an area after a while, and it was practical for them to move on to another region where more food supplies were available. So the government operated from different parts of the country, and indeed it was not unusual for parliament to sit in cities other than London. But by the end of the century, the government was gradually becoming separated from the more social aspects of the court and beginning to be permanently based at Westminster. As the country's affairs became more complex, so it became necessary to have the means of dealing with them on a permanent basis in a central place.

Chaucer was occupied primarily as a professional civil servant, and in this capacity he held a large number of different posts in the course of his life. As a young man he was sent abroad on diplomatic missions and we can imagine that his knowledge of languages, keen sense of verbal nuances and awareness of different human attitudes would have made him an admirable diplomat. Links with the continent of Europe were many in the fourteenth century. From the time of the Norman Conquest (1066) when William the Conqueror brought over to England many Norman knights, rewarding them with territory in England, many families had retained connections with France and noble families long settled in England considered that they had territorial claims to parts of France. But apart from this, there was much coming and going by merchants, by learned men and scholars, by churchmen and by pilgrims. Many educated people had learned Latin and knew French, so that they were able to travel around on the Continent without much difficulty from the point of view of language. Chaucer went to Italy as well as to

France and Spain. He knew French well, since it was spoken in the English court (Edward III knew very little English), and he learned some Italian, though he seems never to have been as fluent in that language as in French.

Chaucer's attachment to the court which provided his livelihood throughout his life must have had its anxieties as well as its satisfactions. Working in close proximity to powerful monarchs and envious courtiers eager for advancement, with all the tensions that would inevitably arise, must have demanded very great tact and restraint. Chaucer is always very reticent in his writings about the immediate circumstances of his life. Now and again he makes a comment which may relate to his experience of the court, mentioning court flattery for example in *The Nun's Priest's Tale*. In *The Knight's Tale*, he indicates indirectly the dangers arising from the imperious ways of dukes and monarchs. In this tale, Duke Theseus decrees that Palamon and Arcite shall be imprisoned indefinitely in a tower, and he has power of life and death over them. When both are found fighting on his territory, he is persuaded not to execute or severely punish them by the pleas of his wife and her sister Emily. It is only the direct efforts of these ladies that prevent him from exercising what is felt to be the natural prerogative of a ruler. It is not surprising that Chaucer does not risk incurring displeasure by commenting on events, or making specific allusions to his everyday experience of life at court.

From the beginning of his career, Chaucer was closely connected with John of Gaunt, Duke of Lancaster, the immensely rich and powerful uncle of Richard II. John of Gaunt owned enormous estates throughout the country and had a splendid palace on the river front in London. During the Peasants' Revolt, much of the intense hostility felt by the peasants was directed against the Duke because he epitomised for them wealth and luxury enjoyed, as it seemed, at their expense. Chaucer wrote one of his earlier poems for John of Gaunt, as an elegy for his wife Blanche. The delicacy with which he performed the difficult task makes the poem a very charming one while at the same time it shows us how Chaucer exercised the utmost tact in working for a royal master. In this poem, *The Book of the Duchess*, Chaucer meets, in a dream, a man dressed in black, who is obviously consumed with grief. In the course of the poem, the stranger explains that he has lost his beloved. The dreamer seems unable to understand what this loss implies and he leads the man in black to speak of her. The poem tells of how the man in black – who is plainly of much higher rank than the dreamer – had gradually come to know and love this lady, how she had at first been reluctant to show him favour, but had at last been persuaded to treat him kindly, and eventually to marry him. As he speaks of this past experience, the man in black recreates an enchanting picture of his beautiful and accomplished lady, who seems to come alive, though she is described in a very stylised way. At the end of the poem he is forced to confront the stark realisation that death has taken her from him for ever, and the dreamer, too, at last understands that she is dead, not merely alienated from her lover. Then he wakes as a bell rings from a nearby castle. The poem makes no attempt to offer consolation: it was not for Chaucer to tell his royal patron not to grieve, or to suggest resignation to God's will, and acceptance of his sorrow. Instead we have an epitaph for Blanche which for a brief time brings her to life again, as a portrait might, created by the sensitive awareness and skill of a poet who knew the need for discretion, especially where his superiors were concerned.

Chaucer's talents – not only as a very competent diplomat and man of affairs, but also as a poet and entertainer – must have been appreciated by his courtly contemporaries. At a time when the production of books was a very costly matter, poets and other writers had to have patrons if they were to survive, and many medieval pictures show authors presenting their works in the form of beautiful books to kings or nobles. Since it was very expensive and difficult to produce even one copy of a book, writers could not live by the sale of their works to the general public as they may now. A king or duke would support a poet by giving him a gift or a pension, but in return the poet would have to take into consideration the tastes of his patron when he wrote. Chaucer's audience may not have been easy to please. Though in writing *Troilus and Criseyde* he had some very serious ideas to communicate, it has been suggested that he had to be careful not to appear to preach to his courtly audience or readers, and in the poem he gracefully suggests that they are experts in the subject of love, with which he is largely concerned, and will be able to judge for themselves, and to imagine for themselves without needing to be told, how the characters feel at various points in the story.

What Chaucer wrote must generally have been what he knew would please a courtly audience. We can imagine him reading his poems aloud, perhaps assuming appropriate voices and accompanying the performance with gestures, to make it more dramatic. He would have amused his hearers by presenting himself – as he does in *The Canterbury Tales* – as an enthusiastic but not very intelligent man, who humbly puts up with the interruption of his story by the uneducated Host, and who is prepared to abandon a tale that does not appear to please the pilgrims and begin another. The real audience in the court of Richard II would have known that Chaucer was not really so simple and uninformed as he represents himself, and would probably have enjoyed the piquant contrast between the man they knew in real life, and the man as he presents himself in his poems. The middle-aged poet who could write so perceptively and subtly about love and human relationships, however, would have given offence if he had claimed to know more about the experience of love than the aristocratic young lovers whom he was addressing, so he assumes a humble guise and presents himself as an ignoramus.

Chaucer's poems in other ways, too, reflect the tastes of the audience for whom he wrote. Just as the literature of our own time mirrors the attitudes and assumptions and way of life of modern society, so medieval literature reflects medieval society, the values and attitudes of courtly people in the fourteenth century, creating for us now an impression of how they saw themselves. In many of his poems Chaucer writes specifically of a social and intellectual élite, though in others he is concerned with people lower in the social scale. Even after six hundred years, we can feel a strong affinity with the world he depicts, while at the same time we recognise how different from his contemporaries we are. In *Troilus and Criseyde*, for example, though we may find the intensity of Troilus's reaction to the experience of falling in love strange in the twentieth century, we can fully sympathise with his agony when his beloved Criseyde is lost to him for ever. He is presented as in many ways an ideal and very typical young courtly lover, extremely brave in battle and utterly devoted to his lady. His love makes him more courageous and noble, more friendly and generous even than before, for these qualities were very highly regarded by the society for which Chaucer wrote. Of course they did not always manage to live up to their ideals, but through Chaucer's writing we are given a sense of the kind of people they wished and tried to be. Likewise Criseyde, though at the end she forsakes Troilus under the stress of circumstances, is in many ways a typical courtly heroine. She is young, beautiful and intensely feminine, but a lively and amusing companion. She is sensitive and affectionate, and her friends admire her charm and poise and good manners. Chaucer shows her attending a dinner party given by one of the sons of King Priam, at which Helen of Troy is present, and when Criseyde leaves before the other guests, we hear them discussing her, behaving just as people often do in similar circumstances at the present day.

So Chaucer in his poems represents the courtliness of the society in which he moved, giving us a clear picture of the elegance and polished manners to which it aspired. Nor are these merely superficial outward forms of behaviour, for Chaucer shows at the same time an underlying courtesy and consideration for others as taken for granted in this society. For example, when Troilus, after Criseyde has had to leave Troy, is taken by his friend Pandarus to stay at the house of another friend so as to distract him from his grief, he is soon in a hurry to go home again. Troilus cannot join in the pleasures of the houseparty because of his sorrow, but Pandarus has agreed that they will stay for a week and he will not hear of Troilus leaving before the week is up, because to do so would insult and hurt the feelings of their host.

Chaucer also shows us how people in other levels of society behave, but the ideal that he presents is a courtly rather than a proletarian one. Of course we cannot assume that court life as Chaucer actually experienced it closely approximated to the ideal. Richard II was a very imperious monarch and in many ways he must have been insufferable. He had come to the throne as a boy of ten and the solemn ritual of the coronation ceremony apparently made a deep impression on him. Throughout his later boyhood and adolescence, the business of government and affairs of state were managed for him by his uncles, which would have created in him an intense expectancy as he waited for the moment when he could rule in his own right. An incident in the Peasants' Revolt must have increased his sense of his own importance: when the country was seething with unrest largely because of the high taxation levied to finance the war with France, a large party of rebels led by Wat Tyler, marched on London. The story is told of how Richard met them at Smithfield and persuaded them to disperse peacefully, assuring them that their grievances would be considered and their suffering alleviated. The crowd, moved by the courage and persuasive manner of the boy king, retreated and the revolt eventually fizzled out.

When Richard was monarch in his own right, he was able to indulge his rather luxurious tastes freely. He loved to wear elaborate and sumptuous robes, made from rich cloths and fine furs, and adorned with splendid jewels. A picture – known as the Wilton diptych – painted in the late fourteenth century and now in the National Gallery, London, shows Richard kneeling before the Virgin Mary and the Christ-child. His robe of golden brocade and his jewelled crown illustrate the richness of late medieval fabrics and the technical skill with which they were woven. The delicacy and beauty of the picture also indicate the skill of fourteenth century artists, while at the same time the diptych gives a vivid impression of a significant aspect of the sensibility of the time: on the one side, behind Richard, stand three holy men, St John the Baptist, and two others who had been kings of England, St Edmund and Edward the Confessor, while opposite the King, the Virgin and child are surrounded by a company of beautiful angels. Richard is seen, therefore, in the context of the spiritual world which was so real to human beings in the fourteenth century, as he prays directly to Mary and Jesus and is supported, as it were, by saints.

The fourteenth century seems to have been a clothes-conscious age; it was not only Richard and his court who felt the appeal of elegant attire, if Chaucer is to be believed. The Canterbury pilgrims' clothes are carefully described, and tell us much about the character of each one. The Knight, to begin with, disregards outward appearances: his eagerness to begin the pilgrimage has prevented him from stopping to change his tunic. The Prioress's brooch and the Wife of Bath's ostentatious outfit show that Chaucer was well aware of the language of dress. In *The Miller's Tale*, the entire costume of the heroine, Alison, is described in detail, and one of her admirers, Absolon, is dressed in what he clearly supposes to be the height of fashion. But it is doubtful if this young man, who seems to pride himself on appearing courtly, would have appeared to be anything but a vulgar imitator of out-of-date fashions. Through his clothes as well as in other ways, Chaucer satirises provincial pretentiousness and human folly.

Expensive clothes, however, showed a worldliness which the Church often found it necessary to reprove. In *The Parson's Tale*, which ends Chaucer's *Canterbury Tales*, the Parson deplores modern fashions; and a contemporary lyric compares the figure of Christ on the cross with the fashionable young man whose hands are elegantly gloved and whose body is dressed in fine clothes, to urge young people to devotion rather than frivolity. Fortunately, fourteenth-century artistic talent found outlets in more permanent art-forms than dress, in – for example – magnificent architecture and stained glass, sculpture and carving. Chaucer's contemporaries were very much aware of the visual and the pictorial, as their art and his poetry clearly show.

Though the court of Edward III and Richard II had its serious concerns, it was also of course a social organisation. Its members, most of them rich and leisured, enjoyed the pleasures which we associate with medieval courtly life: hunting and hawking and tournaments were enjoyable outdoor activities, mentioned in Chaucer's most courtly poems, *The Book of the Duchess* and *The Knight's Tale*. Though life in winter must have been difficult and uncomfortable, as Chaucer's contemporary, the unidentified author of *Sir Gawain and the Green Knight* makes clear in that poem, the coming of spring and summer brought joyful release from the hardships of winter and medieval poems often begin in a springtime setting, as does the *General Prologue* to *The Canterbury Tales*. Chaucer himself speaks of his love of going out into the fields in early summer to admire the daisies that make them beautiful again. Dancing was another pastime much enjoyed by courtly people, as Chaucer indicates in *The Book of the Duchess*, in *Troilus and Criseyde*, in *The Franklin's Tale*, and elsewhere. Dancing implied ordered and stylised movement and could be thought of as symbolising the joy and harmony of heaven. It could also, however, have less spiritual connotations: the Wife of Bath, that most earthy of the Canterbury Pilgrims, is said by Chaucer to know all about the 'olde daunce' of love. The idea of dancing also suggests music, and some of the medieval dance music that has survived conveys a sense of celebration and energetic, light-hearted enjoyment. Music, of course, played a vital part in church worship, and the plain-song or Gregorian chant, often sung to this day in the Christian church, continues the tradition in which Chaucer's

Prioress and the friars singing in the chancel (in *The Miller's Tale*) were brought up. Music meant much to medieval people: they considered it the highest of the arts because, even more than the dance, it was representative of the divine harmony. For them it was expressive of the most intense ecstacy, and when it accompanied such ritualistic activities as the beginning of a tournament or the bringing of the food for a feast, hearts were lifted high (as the *Gawain* poet tells us) at the stirring sounds.

It is not surprising, therefore, that the courtly way of life tended to be idealised in the literature of the fourteenth century, even if the reality was often rather different from the ideal. At the present day we are perhaps more ready to confront and represent the darker realities of twentieth century life than to enshrine our ideals in great literature. We live in a less optimistic age, and our outlook, limited in the main to the things of this world, is a sombre one. For medieval man, however, the celebration of his vision of earthly life at its noblest and best in courtly literature was counterbalanced by an ever-present awareness of human sinfulness. Both earthly happiness and the hope of salvation were tempered by fear of damnation and everlasting torment; now we mainly take a shorter view, in which fear for the future is offset by the material satisfactions of the present moment.

Chaucer's London

Living most of his life in London gave Chaucer an opportunity for wide and diverse experience in what was both the seat of government and a great cultural centre. He was fortunate in being the son of a prosperous merchant who could give him a good start in life, both in terms of education and by placing him in a noble household which offered opportunities for social advancement.

Chaucer's father's house was close to the river Thames, so business transactions could be conducted from the family home while the wines were unloaded on the quay. Close by, and close to the river, were many large mansions or 'inns' belonging to nobles, while a maze of narrow lanes further back from the water-front was the site of poorer houses and little shops. Not far away was London Bridge, on which in Chaucer's boyhood there were no less than one hundred and thirty eight shops, as well as a chapel dedicated to St Thomas Becket, the 'hooly blisful martir' of the *General Prologue* to *The Canterbury Tales*. Because London was a busy port as well as the capital, many foreign merchants from different parts of Europe had houses there, and in one quarter there was a colony of weavers from Flanders. The various trades tended to have their own particular quarters: the Poultry, for example, was where sellers of poultry and some other kinds of meat had their shops and stalls, and the Peltry was where the tanners processed their hides and skins. The city must often have been an evil-smelling place, for waste-disposal was a perennial problem. The Shambles, where beasts were slaughtered to provide meat, produced much waste which had to be transported in carts to the Fleet ditch – a twenty-foot wide ditch that ran into the Thames – until at the end of the century more efficient arrangements were devised. With its narrow streets and rather primitive sanitation, London must have been an unhealthy place to live in, but as a capital city it must also have been a lively and interesting centre of activity where there was always something going on.

Though the City of London itself was surrounded by walls, with gates which were closed each night at curfew time (as in *Troilus and Criseyde*, V.1117–80), there were many important buildings outside the walls, as well as suburbs. One of the king's palaces was situated at Westminster, and close to it was Westminster Hall, in which parliament met. Richard II had its old roof replaced by the magnificent hammerbeam roof which can still be seen today. Presumably Chaucer speaks from experience when he mentions a parliamentary sitting in *Troilus and Criseyde* (IV.141–3) and he must have sat in Westminster Hall when he was Knight of the Shire for Kent in 1386. Westminster Abbey, near by, had a garden in which stood the small house where Chaucer spent the last months of his life.

There were monks at the Abbey, and elsewhere in London there were a number of convents and priories for monks, nuns and friars belonging to the various religious orders. At the Charterhouse there were eighteen Carthusian monks, for instance, while Greyfriars was inhabited by Franciscans. London was full of churches, of which St Paul's Cathedral, with its great spire, must have been the most impressive. Its large nave was used on weekdays for business purposes of various kinds, which still left a very extensive area for church services: religion and everyday life were virtually inseparable. Richard II's palace at Westminster had a great chamber for court business and ceremonial, at one side of which was a small chapel, and this also adjoined the king's bedchamber. A window was constructed to allow Richard to hear mass from his bed.

Much of the business of government was conducted in and from the palace, but the Tower of London was also a royal residence. Here large supplies of weapons were stored, and prisoners were accommodated. There were other prisons at Ludgate and Newgate, while debtors were sent to the Fleet Prison. Law-breakers and wrong-doers were not always imprisoned, however: they might be held in the stocks in the street or in the market place, so that people could take note of them and avoid dishonest traders. London had its recognised seamy side, represented by the Stews (the houses of prostitutes) across the river from the City, in Southwark.

Tournaments provided more respectable forms of entertainment, taking place in various parts of the city, and Chaucer had the difficult task of organising the stands for the Great Jousts in Smithfield in 1390. All sorts of sports, such as archery (a useful skill encouraged by the authorities), wrestling, ball games and cock-fighting took place; and religious processions and pageants of various kinds provided interest and colour for citizens and travellers.

War and chivalry

Chaucer was born at a time when England was at war with France, in the so-called Hundred Years' War which continued throughout his lifetime, as England struggled to retain and to extend her possessions in France. As a young man, Chaucer was trained as a matter of course in the use of arms and was actually taken prisoner in France while participating in a campaign, though later he was ransomed. Thus he had direct personal experience of war, a topic which figures in a number of his poems.

Attitudes to war in the Middle Ages were different from those held by many people today. It was considered the duty of a king to extend his territory, and in an age when disease, accident or hardship inevitably carried off a high proportion of the population, the loss of young men's lives incurred by military campaigns did not appear as shocking as it does to most people now. Knights welcomed the opportunity to win honour and fame by their courageous exploits; those of lower rank looked forward to enriching themselves with plunder and booty. Few people seem to have worried about the plight of the civilian population in areas ravaged by war, or in towns beseiged by enemy armies: such disasters had to be accepted as the natural consequence of man's sinful nature. But Chaucer seems to have been well aware that there was more to war than the excitement of battle and the triumph of conquest, and in *The Knight's Tale* he indicates some of the other things that are involved. At the beginning of this Tale, we see Duke Theseus returning home with his bride, only to be greeted by a long line of griefstricken ladies, whose husbands have been killed in battle and whose bodies they have been unable to see appropriately buried. To right the wrong that has been done to them, Duke Theseus immediately sets off to besiege the city of Thebes, and very soon sacks it. The dead bodies of the Thebans are at once ransacked for spoil by the pillagers, and under the pile of dead bodies are found two young men, Palamon and Arcite, still alive, who are taken prisoner. So, in order to give justice to the mourning ladies, many other people have to die or suffer: one person's gain is another person's loss, in war and also in peace, as the story subsequently shows. The noble Duke will accept no ransom for the young men – though ransom-money was regarded as a significant source of revenue in medieval war – and imprisons them in a tower indefinitely. Later on in the story, we are shown some other aspects of war in more symbolic manner in the Temple of Mars, to whom Arcite prays. Though the glamour of war may figure prominently in medieval society, here it is offset by a comprehensive picture of what war really involves. The treachery and brutality and horror which are inevitable are emphasised: war implies violence and in consequence suffering.

However, Duke Theseus is a just, even merciful and efficient ruler, and when earlier in the story he discovers Palamon and Arcite fighting like wild beasts for the love of the beautiful Emily, he spares their lives and arranges that their quarrel shall be settled in a year's time, by means of a great tournament. In the fourteenth century, chivalry was the means by which the aggressive instincts of young men could be controlled and canalised. The tournament provided useful training and practice for actual warfare, and it also allowed the settling of disputes and quarrels between knights. So, in due course, Palamon and Arcite return with their supporters for the tournament which is to decide who is to win the hand of Emily. We see the splendour of chivalry as all the knights arrive with their heralds and banners, weapons and armour for the contest. Duke Theseus is enthusiastically acclaimed by all because he declares that the fight shall not be to the death, but only to decide who is the stronger. So the contestants enter the splendid lists that have been prepared as arena for the tournament. Chaucer must have been writing from direct experience in describing the lists. In 1390, in his capacity of Clerk of the Works, he was himself responsible for the organisation of the lists for a great joust at Smithfield in London, and he must have been familiar with such events, if on a smaller scale, all his life. But despite or perhaps because of his early experience in France, chivalry and tales of chivalric adventure do not seem to have greatly appealed to him.

Chivalry, however, played a large part in medieval life. Chaucer's Knight, the first of the Canterbury pilgrims to be described in the *General Prologue*, is not only a living embodiment of chivalry, but at the same time one of the few pilgrims to be idealised by Chaucer. He has taken part in a great many battles and sieges, and fought for his faith, as a crusader. Despite his many campaigns, he is neither ruthless, aggressive nor belligerent, but a devout Christian, and a peace-maker when a quarrel breaks out between two of the pilgrims. The medieval knight saw his profession as perfectly compatible with his religion and indeed chivalry was closely connected with Christianity. Before he was made a knight, it was usual for a young man to keep a vigil in church, and the ceremony of dubbing was associated with religious ritual. Putting on his armour, the knight might think of himself as putting on the armour of God; and the poet Langland (?1330–?1400) (and other writers too), thought of Christ as a knight, putting on the armour of humanity to joust against the devil for mankind's salvation.

The ideals of chivalry involved, above all else, courage and loyalty. The knight should value his life 'no more than a bunch of cherries'. Such an ideal could be pushed to extraordinary lengths, as in an incident recorded by Chaucer's contemporary Froissart (?1337–*c*.1410) in writing of the war with France. The blind King John of Bohemia, supporting the French side, wished to strike one blow for his cause, and asked the knights of his household to enable him to do so by leading him into battle. They lashed their horses' bridles together, with the king in the middle, and together dashed forward to the attack. Inevitably, all were killed. When they were found later, their horses were still bound together. Their loyalty to their king and their courage kept them united in death. Medieval romances, for example the stories of King Arthur and his knights, are full of comparable, if less spectacular, instances of reckless courage. Sir Launcelot fighting with the treacherous, contemptible Sir Meliagaunt, (in Malory's *Le Morte Darthur* (1470)), sets aside some of his armour and fights with one hand tied behind his back, to give his antagonist a better chance. Sir Gawain (in *Sir Gawain and the Green Knight*) after bravely taking on the challenge of the Green Knight to spare the king, and after beheading this alarming figure, sets off for what seems certain death at the Green Chapel a year later in fulfilment on his promise, though fortunately he survives.

One of the main objects of the knight was to gain honour, as we see in *The Franklin's Tale*. In this, Arveragus leaves his bride to go overseas to King Arthur's court, in order to win honour by his deeds of prowess, and having done so, returns home satisfied, his mission accomplished. A knight's honour consisted in the reputation for courage thus gained, but Chaucer shows in *The Franklin's Tale* that there are still more vital values in life: 'Truth is the highest thing that man may keep' – in other words, personal integrity is even more important than what people think of you. It is better to be true to your word, to keep your promises, even if you suffer loss and humiliation and are despised as a result, than to be highly regarded by your peers. Arveragus makes a great personal sacrifice for the sake of truth, thus risking the loss of his honour, but in the end, all turns out well for him.

Medieval society was regarded as being divided into three main groups or 'estates', of which the knights were the first, with the church as the second main group and other people – the laity – as the third. Chaucer had many friends who were knights, so naturally he thought well of this social group, but he was not the only writer to do so. Like many others before him, he attributed noble characteristics to the typical knight. Langland in *Piers Plowman* emphasises the value of the knight's contribution to the well-being of his community: he guards the land from attack, so that crops can be grown by ploughmen and husbandmen, and his hunting rids it of predators that would destroy the crops. Though medieval men suffered much from war – whether directly when attacked or besieged, or indirectly when taxed severely to pay for campaigns – they accepted fighting as an inevitable condition of life. Life was itself seen as one long battle against the world, the flesh and the devil for the medieval Christian.

In *Troilus and Criseyde*, Chaucer gives a lively picture of the conventions and conditions of medieval warfare. He depicts the siege of the ancient city of Troy, later burnt by the Greeks, who entered it by means of a large wooden horse which the Trojans themselves dragged in. Despite the siege, life goes on very much as normal in Troy. Friends meet, dinner parties are given, and the love affair of Troilus and Criseyde is of paramount importance in their lives. Fighting goes on, but it takes the form of chivalric encounters between individual warriors, who sally forth from city and camp, fight each other and go back. Often truces are arranged, so that the inhabitants can go in and out of the city, and supplies can be brought in from the surrounding countryside. Though not all medieval sieges were like this, it is clear that chivalry made it sometimes possible to conduct hostilities in a curiously ordered, gentlemanly way, very different from the total warfare of the present time. The medieval warrior met his opponent face to face and fought man to man, often respecting the courage of his adversary and having regard to the rules of fair play.

Training in the military arts was an essential part of a boy's education if he belonged to the knightly class and he was often considered old enough to fight when in his early teens. The Black Prince experienced his first battle in 1346 at the age of fourteen: his father, Edward III, consented to his participation, seeing the need for the boy to win his spurs, despite the danger. In *The Knight's Tale*, Palamon and Arcite are young boys when they are rescued from a pile of bodies after the siege of Thebes; and Troilus, though regarded as a notable warrior, appears to be in his late teens when the story opens.

But though such early participation in serious warfare was taken for granted, and young men were eager to prove themselves and win their spurs, it was sometimes the case that knights were reluctant to take up their hereditary titles. The cost of providing and maintaining a troop of men, as the knight was obliged to do when his king or overlord required it, and the expense of his suit of armour, was more than some men felt they could afford. In Chaucer's time, a suit of armour usually consisted partly of flexible chain mail and partly of metal plates to protect vulnerable parts of the body: the image of the knight in shining armour still has its romantic appeal for the modern mind, as it did in the Middle Ages. In *Troilus and Criseyde*, we see Criseyde watching Troilus riding back victorious from battle; she is deeply moved by the noble sight, even though his armour has been much hacked about in the encounter.

The Crusades, the military expeditions undertaken by Christians to recapture the Holy Land from Islam in the eleventh, twelfth and thirteenth centuries, had of course come to an end when Chaucer was writing, but he nevertheless depicts the Knight as having taken part in religious wars, in Lithuania and elsewhere. That the Knight has done so is quite compatible with his being one of the few pilgrims to be represented as an idealised figure.

The Church and religion

It is hard for many modern readers to appreciate the enormous part that the Church, and all that it implied, played in most people's lives. Though we are given an indication of the comprehensive range of functions within the organisation as a whole by the number of pilgrims depicted by Chaucer who are connected with the Church, we have to read between the lines, too, to discover the extent to which religion permeated everybody's everyday life. Yet without some understanding of this fact, it is hard to come to a full understanding and appreciation of Chaucer's work.

A first reading of the *General Prologue* to *The Canterbury Tales* makes it very clear that by no means all the pilgrims are saintly characters. Indeed, most of those directly connected with the Church can be seen to be failing markedly to live up to the ideals to which they should aspire. All, however, even the most sinful, the most neglectful of their religious duties, are believers. Chaucer wrote in an age of faith, when there was virtually no alternative to belief. The teaching of the Church so permeated everyday life, and the belief that it inculcated was so unchallenged by science that the Christian world-view was universally accepted. The teaching of the Church was that life itself is a pilgrimage, from the cradle to the grave, a journey that ended not just with death but with the Last Judgment, a very real and frightening prospect for Chaucer's contemporaries.

Let us begin with the implications of this belief. It was a belief that naturally inculcated anxiety and fear: the fourteenth century was a frightening age – like many others – to live in. It seemed to many people living then that unmistakable signs of God's anger were apparent in the world around them, and to individual fears of death and judgment was added the alarming thought that the end of the world was at hand. In 1348 there was an outbreak of bubonic plague in Europe, which soon spread to England, resulting in the Black Death of 1348–9. This terrifying epidemic, from which there seemed to be no escape, and for which there were no remedies, killed a very large proportion of the population. The horror of the disease itself and the fear that it inspired were only a part of the total disaster: it led to widespread social disruption as the countryside was depopulated and few active people were left to cultivate the fields and provide food for those who survived. As in the nineteenth century, when outbreaks of cholera in England were regarded by many people as indications of the anger of God, the plague was seen as a sign of divine displeasure, in an age when ignorance, superstition and credulity were predominant.

Chaucer had no wish to write about such morbid topics, but the fact that his pilgrims from many different walks of life are all going to the Shrine of St Thomas at Canterbury suggests how widespread spiritual anxiety was. It was an age of intense devotion, one form of which consisted in visits to the shrines of saints, such as the 'holy blisful martyr', who, says Chaucer, had helped the pilgrims when they were sick. People believed that visits to the shrines of saints would not only be pleasing to God, but would also enable them to avail themselves of the spiritual power of the saints and martyrs. Many psychosomatic diseases must have been cured by such pilgrimages, but at the same time, many impostures were practised by those who found ways to exploit the pilgrims. At Canterbury, hen's blood was sold as the authentic blood of St Thomas the Martyr, and Chaucer makes it very obvious that the relics his Pardoner carries with him are far from being genuine.

Pilgrimages, however, though their prime purpose was of course religious, were – as we see from *The Canterbury Tales* – often enjoyable excursions, too. The Wife of Bath has been on many; and the modern reader can still be amazed at the enormous distances medieval pilgrims travelled, when there were no means of travel faster than a horse, and no accurate maps to guide the traveller. But the pilgrimage gave people the opportunity for seeing new scenes and for the sort of enjoyable interchange that Chaucer describes, as his pilgrims set out, tell their stories and argue or exchange points of view with each other as they go. As they travelled, on foot or on horseback, knowing that they were engaged in a worthy spiritual undertaking, they could let themselves go a little and perhaps even forget in the enjoyment of the holiday atmosphere, the anxieties, worldly and spiritual, perpetually hanging over their lives.

They were likely, however, to be reminded of death and judgment whenever they entered a church, for there they would find carvings, sculptures and wall paintings reiterating – as did the services and sermons, too – that there would be no escape. Often over the doorway there would be a representation of Christ in Judgment; or on the chancel arch, above the heads of the congregation at the point where the main part of the church (the nave) was separated from the chancel, (the most sacred part of the building) paintings would depict the weighing of souls to determine their final destination. On Christ's left-hand side there would be a frighteningly grotesque picture of hell's mouth, like the jaws of an enormous monster, ready to swallow up the wicked into everlasting torment, while devils with three-pronged forks helped to toss them into the flames of hell, or carried the sinful souls away on their backs. On the other side of the picture, the blessed were shown, being conducted by angels to everlasting bliss in the New Jerusalem, the heavenly city. Such pictures were regarded as a useful form of instruction, for in the fourteenth century the Bible was not freely available, as it is now, to all who could read. The medieval Christian was dependent upon his parish priest for religious teaching and what the priest taught normally depended upon the readings selected for the day, in accordance with the Christian year. The medieval church-goer would thus hear certain stories from the Old and New Testaments but might never hear other parts of the Bible. His attention would be especially directed to the particularly emotive and poignant episodes which centred on the birth of Christ, and also on his crucifixion, and might be invited to contemplate with fervent devotion this supreme example of love and suffering, which was frequently represented in art and literature. In the fourteenth century, love seems always to be associated with suffering, as we see in many of Chaucer's poems and in the work of other writers.

Chaucer does not say very much about this aspect of the spiritual and imaginative life of his age, but in *The Summoner's Tale*, a wicked summoner is carried off to hell by a devil, to the great satisfaction of one of his intended victims. However, the reality of death and judgment for medieval people meant that there was an underlying seriousness in their attitude to literature which is significant for an understanding of Chaucer's poems. At the very end of *The Canterbury Tales*, Chaucer, unable to finish his great project, and apparently confronting death, repents of and rejects those of his tales and works which might be construed as having a sinful tendency. His anxiety about his own soul has its counterpart in his concern for the possible corruption of the souls of others, which may be held against him at the last. It presupposes an attitude unfamiliar to us now, but apparent at several points in *The Canterbury Tales*. The pilgrims often want to hear 'som moral thyng, that we may leere [learn]', they want tales of 'doctrine and sentence' – in other words, instructive tales which will be spiritually beneficial, not simply entertaining. In an age when information was so hard to come by, there was a great thirst for instruction and a desire for what would encourage spiritual growth and lead the reader or hearer further along the path to heaven. So medieval literature usually starts from a serious idea and often seeks to communicate deeper meanings than may appear on the surface, instead of – as modern literature so often does – starting with a character or group of characters and attempting to present a 'slice of life'.

Medieval people saw this world as a spiritual battleground in which there was a constant, ongoing conflict between the forces of good and evil. They were not only beset by the actual dangers of accident and disease, fire and flood, famine and war, but they were threatened by spiritual perils in a world where angels and demons were ever active. They tended to see good and evil in terms of such beings, and for them the world of spiritual reality was in a sense more intensely real than the tangible mundane world about them. The very real miseries of life in the Middle Ages help us to appreciate how it was that people felt as they did. With no effective medicine, no anaesthetics, no insurance against disaster, no birth-control and when fifty per cent of infants died before reaching the age of five, this world was a grim place for many people. Riches might make life more comfortable, but they could not protect people from pain or sudden death. One of Chaucer's earliest surviving poems is his elegy for Blanche, the young wife of John of Gaunt, who died in 1369 aged only twenty one. His contemporaries often consoled themselves with the thought that the rich and powerful had to die and face judgment and decay in the grave just as the poor did, and also with the belief that this world could not be all – there must be another realm beyond, as the Bible teaches, to make up for the miseries that human beings have to endure in this. Palamon and Arcite in *The Knight's Tale* ponder on these matters, for example when Palamon speaks of the unfairness of man's lot; for man has been given instincts akin to those of the animals, yet if he allows himself to indulge his desires, he will be punished for his sins. Arcite, however, as he lies dying, does not look forward to the joys of heaven, and though the Tale ends on a reassuring note, it does not radiate confidence throughout.

Medieval religion naturally shaped and affected people's attitudes to life and death in many ways. It also affected their lives in more mundane ways, too. The Church was the great employer, and the nuns and monks, friars and pardoners, summoners and parsons represented on Chaucer's pilgrimage suggest some of the different professional or vocational roles which it provided. The church building in each parish would have been the main meeting place for the inhabitants, where they would congregate not only on Sundays but also often on week-days. The Church provided not only forms of worship, nourishing the spiritual and devotional life of the congregation, but teaching and, in a sense, entertainment too. Parish priests and itinerant preachers such as the Pardoner taught their congregations and enlivened their instruction with colourful denunciations of sin – *The Pardoner's Prologue and Tale* gives an example of the kinds of approach and techniques with which fourteenth-century congregations were enlightened. The Church was also a great patron of the arts, and medieval men and women must have derived pleasure from the rich, bold colours of the stained glass windows, from the wall paintings and statues, from the gargoyles and carvings that adorned the walls of the church buildings, inside and out. It was a meeting place for the exchange of news and gossip, as well as a place for spiritual experience. *The Miller's Tale* tells us how Absolon, the parish clerk, enjoys his parochial duties among the pretty young women, and obviously makes the most of the opportunity it gives him to look at them in a lustful way. The Church was also the originator and in one respect the organiser of the miracle or mystery plays which were often performed on the Feast of Corpus Christi, plays which the Wife of Bath enjoyed, and in which Absolon took the part of Herod. They dealt with the whole history of the world from the very beginning – before even the creation of men – to the Final Judgment, and their main purpose was to remind the audience of Christ's death on the cross to save mankind, and to celebrate and commemorate the institution of the sacrament of the Last Supper by means of which the Christian soul is nourished and strengthened.

The medieval Church was, however, as Chaucer makes clear in the *General Prologue*, a very corrupt institution – perhaps inevitably, in view of its vast organisation and inclusiveness. Though the Church was very powerful, it was not without its critics. The Lollards, originally followers of John Wycliffe (1329–84) were the most outspoken, and Chaucer – who is, of course, outspoken in his criticism in his own way – had friends who were both Lollards and knights.

In *The Canterbury Tales* Chaucer draws attention to the greedy self-indulgence and immorality of many of the ecclesiastical figures on the pilgrimage. When large numbers of the population were vowed to celibacy as members of religious orders, living in monasteries and convents, pressures and problems were inevitable. Not surprisingly, one outlet for such pressures was anti-feminist writing. If Eve had not eaten the apple, she and Adam would not have been cast out of the Garden of Eden, and mankind would not for ever have been excluded from paradise, and fallen. All women, daughters of Eve, could therefore be regarded as potentially dangerous to men, instruments of the devil who might imperil men's souls.

Though the downfall of mankind was blamed on the disobedience of Eve, the balance was restored – in the eyes of medieval people – by the Virgin Mary, the second Eve, who as the mother of Christ was the means of salvation. Devotion to the Virgin Mary channelled the love and tenderness, perhaps otherwise repressed, of medieval Christians, and as she increasingly became a cult figure, chapels in her honour were often added to cathedrals and churches, statues carved and lyrics written. She was the ideal young mother, often lovingly portrayed with her child in her arms, and men prayed to her to intercede for them before God. Thus she created as it were a pattern and a role for women: we can see from

Chaucer's poems how their function is often to intercede with men to have pity and to show mercy. In *The Knight's Tale*, the Queen and Emily beg Theseus to spare Palamon and Arcite; in *The Wife of Bath's Tale*, the Queen pleads with King Arthur to spare the life of a knight who had raped a young girl, and to give him another chance.

This belief that the Virgin Mary was the second Eve, sent to redress the evil brought into the world at the Fall, indicates another aspect of medieval life, the tendency to think in symmetrical patterns. The first Adam's sin had to be counterbalanced by the second Adam's – Christ's – sacrifice; the first Eve's disobedience was offset by Mary's acceptance of God's purpose for her. Though these patterns are more apparent in the medieval drama and religious writing than in most of Chaucer's work, they underlie the commonly accepted attitudes to life of Chaucer's contemporaries.

Such ways of organising ideas helped to make them more easily remembered, no doubt, at a time when men had to rely on their memories much more than we do now. They liked to group concepts and to contrast and counterbalance them: the Seven Deadly Sins, which play a considerable part in *The Parson's Tale*, and a lesser but perhaps more lively one in *The Pardoner's Tale*, are an example of how such grouping of ideas helped the systematic communication of information. The preacher could remember schematically the instruction that he wished to give, and then could enliven it by illustrating it with colourful examples, stories ·and anecdotes. We see this happening in *The Pardoner's Tale* in particular, and in *The Nun's Priest's Tale* the cock, Chauntecleer, in informing his wife Pertelote of the danger of disregarding warning dreams, supports his argument with well chosen examples of appropriate incidents.

The acceptance of the belief that the universe is in God's hand and entirely within his control had significant implications, an understanding of which makes many of Chaucer's tales more comprehensible. First of all, it was generally accepted (though *The Knight's Tale* suggests that Chaucer had some intellectual doubts about this belief) that God's loving providence governed the world, as Duke Theseus, a trustworthy figure, asserts at the end of *The Knight's Tale*, despite what have seemed to be appearances to the contrary. And God's purpose for each individual human being, and the destiny which ensues for him, must be accepted in the belief that God's all-seeing wisdom and love has decided what is best for each individual soul. So obedience, patience and acceptance are vitally necessary. Man cannot see God's entire purpose; he must accept that what God has decreed, even if it involves suffering in this life, is ultimately best for him and will lead to salvation and perhaps the bliss of heaven in the end. We see Dorigen in *The Franklin's Tale* questioning God's wisdom in allowing the rocks off the coast of Brittany to imperil the lives of sailors; and then, when the rocks are made to disappear by magic, we see that Dorigen's lack of patience and reluctance to accept the world as God has made it involves a greater danger. When the rocks are invisible, they constitute a worse hazard than when they can be seen and avoided. Disobedience, impatience and lack of trust invite disaster; acceptance and faith in the ultimately loving providence of God are essential.

Medieval men saw God's purpose being worked out in this world through various agents. Through the planets, God exerted control over human destinies ('The stars rain influences'), affecting the fortunes of nations as well as of individuals, and even having their effect upon plants and minerals as well. The study of astrology was a serious science, and Chaucer makes frequent allusion to it in his works. In *Troilus and Criseyde* and in *The Knight's Tale* in particular we see that the operation of the planets affects the lives of human beings in significant ways, but in each case under the ultimate control of God.

Another agent of God was Fortune, often depicted as a female figure with a wheel which she turned. This image derived from a late classical goddess, Fortuna, and it communicated effectively the keen medieval sense of the uncertainties of life. Fortune brought about the chance happenings, the incidents and accidents, large or small, of daily life which constantly confront us with temptations, problems and choices to make. Fortune could also be seen as operating on a larger time-scale: the pictures of her with her wheel frequently show kings being carried up on it as it turned, reaching at the top the height of their power and success, and then being tumbled down to disaster and death as the wheel went on turning.

Nature, too, was often depicted as a female figure, God's deputy, bringing about the successive changes in the natural world such as the seasons, and presiding over such processes as generation – the mating of animals and birds, for example. So Chaucer portrays her in *The Parliament of Fowls*, where she is seen supervising the choosing of mates by the birds on St Valentine's Day, and dealing sympathetically with their problems of rivalry and decision making. But though Nature is thus seen as a benevolent figure, helping to work out the purpose of God, nature in the more general sense in which we use it now meant something very different to Chaucer's contemporaries. In the Middle Ages, the countryside was often frightening, and to be alone in wild places, far from civilisation, was not regarded as a pleasant experience. Chaucer's contemporary, the author of *Sir Gawain and the Green Knight*, makes this very clear when Sir Gawain is going on a long journey through the wintry countryside, 'with no-one to speak to but God and his horse', to find the Green Chapel and meet the Green Knight. The harsh, cold conditions of the journey and the loneliness make him overjoyed when he at last reaches a beautiful castle which offers all the comforts and – it would seem – the security of civilisation. So heaven was depicted as a city or castle, a place of refuge from the miseries of this life, and the image of the garden provided an image of nature at its most attractive. The medieval garden is walled or fenced, excluding the dangers to be encountered in the open countryside and including carefully cultivated flowers and trees – nature tamed and ordered and regulated. The garden was a symbol, moreover, of the place of significant encounters and happenings: Eve was tempted in the garden of Eden, for example. In Chaucer's poems, we see Dorigen's unfortunate meeting with the young squire Aurelius taking place in a garden in *The Franklin's Tale*; in *The Merchant's Tale*, May and her lover Damian make an assignation, which takes place with remarkable consequences, in a walled garden. In the *Knight's Tale*, Palamon and Arcite see the lovely Emily walking in her garden and though they are separated from her by their imprisonment within a tower, their psychological encounter, their instant falling in love with her, is made more striking by taking place where it does. So in *Troilus and Criseyde*, too, some significant experiences take place in Criseyde's garden, which lends its atmosphere to the feeling being generated by the poem.

Men's lives, then, were generally seen as being shaped and regulated by God's providence, working itself out through His various channels of power. There was, however, controversy as to the extent to which man had free-will and to what extent God had predestined each individual soul to heaven or hell. Chaucer alludes to this argument in *The Nun's Priest's Tale*, and deals with it at greater length in *Troilus and Criseyde*. Chaucer, influenced by the late Roman writer Boethius (*d.* AD524), seems to have come to the conclusion that man does have free-will, and can freely choose how he will respond and act in the various situations with which life confronts him; but then again, God already knows what choice he will make, for God is outside time, and sees past, present and future as co-existent in His eternal present.

This is the conclusion implicit in *Troilus and Criseyde* and elsewhere in Chaucer's writing, but it is difficult to pin down Chaucer's religious beliefs with any great exactness or certainty, generally speaking. Amongst his earliest works is a poem in honour of the Virgin Mary, and his last work ends with his Retractation, already mentioned, in which he repudiates such of his works as are conducive to sin. He undoubtedly accepted the religious beliefs of his age, though he probably had difficulty in making them accord with some of the problems with which life confronted him, as does Palamon in *The Knight's Tale*. His outlook on life was predominantly a secular one, and though religion, in various ways, often entered into his writing, it does not dominate it.

Love, sex and marriage

Throughout his career as a writer, Chaucer seems to have been fascinated and perplexed by the subject of love and the problems to which it gives rise. He shows it in many different guises, from the noble, faithful, unselfish love of Troilus for Criseyde, to the shamelessly lustful desire of Nicholas for Alison in *The Miller's Tale*. At its best, love appears as an all-absorbing passion which makes the lover sick and weak with longing for his lady, dedicating himself to her service, hoping to win her favour, and to receive her grace and be treated with mercy. The relationship in some ways resembles the feudal relationship between a man and his overlord, for the lover must be humble and obedient. Such love cannot change; and it inevitably brings suffering with it, even if in the end the lover is rewarded with his lady's hand in marriage.

The emotion experienced by the true lover often expresses itself in songs, which represent in stylised, poetic form his ecstasy or the intensity of his longing. It may make him weep or even faint, for such powerful sensations are necessarily also expressed by bodily symptoms. At the same time, it ennobles his whole nature, making him braver and better in every way.

If, however, the love is true love, it cannot simply be set aside if the lady chooses a rival lover, and in both *The Parliament of Fowls* and *The Knight's Tale* Chaucer confronts a situation in which rivals compete for their beloved. In such poems, he makes us aware of the complexity of human experience, and of the impossibility of finding satisfactory solutions for the problems of living and loving. Though deep and faithful love is a splendid thing in many ways, it has its absurdities, too, for it places the unsuccessful lover in an impossible situation.

Chaucer is very well aware, however, that many human beings are less high-minded and patient than such lovers as Troilus, Palamon and Arcite, and the tercel eagles in *The Parliament of Fowls*; and he shows us others, such as Diomede in *Troilus and Criseyde*, Nicholas in *The Miller's Tale*, and the 'lower' birds in *The Parliament of Fowls*, who do not believe in patient service, but quickly find practical ways to possess their beloved. Though the noble lover does not commit adultery (Troilus and Criseyde, though they do not marry, do not commit adultery, because neither is married to someone else), Chaucer shows a number of adulterous situations, for he knew that they occurred often enough in real life. Instead of condemning them, he shows them as only arising where the characters are *not* noble and admirable.

Marriage was the ambition of the noble lover, as we see in *The Book of the Duchess*. But after marriage, the situation of the lover and his lady was reversed, and the expectation was that the wife would obey her husband. In *The Franklin's Tale* Arveragus and Dorigen enter into an unconventional arrangement, in which only the outward appearance of submission on the part of the wife is preserved, and she retains the autonomy that she had enjoyed during their courtship. When problems arise because of her foolish promise to her admirer, Aurelius, in her husband's absence, Dorigen eventually has to confess to Arveragus that she is in deep trouble and ask him to solve her problem. In the end, she has to submit to his judgment. What may seem to us to be a satisfactory, modern, almost ideal marriage-relationship is shown to be impractical after all; but the relationship of Dorigen and Arveragus is perfect in the mutual love and trust on which it is based.

In *The Clerk's Tale* of patient Griselda, we see a wife submitting to the consequences of her husband's obsession with testing her, with exemplary patience and obedience. To the modern reader, the demands of her husband and her immediate and total compliance seem ridiculous, but though she submits as a wife was expected to do, she wins a moral victory in the end. Chaucer's sympathy for women is everywhere apparent in his writing, and particularly when young women are married to elderly husbands. In *The Wife of Bath's Prologue*, he shows that they may find their own ways of dealing with such unsatisfactory marriage situations.

Sexual love is not, of course, the only kind of love which Chaucer depicts in his poems. Love for God and for the Virgin Mary also find a place, beginning with the early poem, 'An A.B.C.', in praise of Mary. In *The Prioress's Tale*, this spiritual love is again exemplified, as is the love of a mother for her child. Chaucer gives noble expression to spiritual aspiration, at the end of *Troilus and Criseyde*, where he urges young people to turn their hearts to God, and love him only – even though the whole poem has been a celebration of the splendour of earthly love.

Throughout his poetic career, Chaucer manifested a sympathy for women, bad as well as good, in contrast with clerical anti-feminist writing which denounced women as evil, and dangerous sources of temptation. Though he could show, as in *The Wife of Bath's Prologue*, that such misogynistic views might sometimes have some justification, it is a deeply understanding, tolerant attitude that constantly emerges; he is able to view women as individuals – faulty, of course, like men – but entitled to happiness and satisfaction in love and marriage, in an age when women's liberation had not been thought of. His exploration of the psychology of love and of sexual experience everywhere reveals his unfailing interest in human nature and the extent of his knowledge of it.

Education and the world of learning

We know very little about Chaucer's formal education, but one thing is certain, that his education did not stop when the time came for him to leave school, for his life-long devotion to books brought him into contact, throughout his life, with new fields of learning, sources of information, and works of literature.

We do not know how Chaucer was taught, or whether he did in fact go to school. He would have learnt to read, in English, at an early age, and then might well have gone on to one of the grammar schools, such as St Paul's, already established in London. There, his education would have concentrated on Latin, until after much intensive study, he had a good grounding in what was regarded as a crucial subject. Both teaching and learning must have been rather hard work, for so few resources were available to assist the process. The rarity and enormous cost of books meant that almost everything had to be learnt by heart – first dictated and then committed to memory. But eventually, after years of effort on both sides and of no sparing of the rod by the teacher, boys acquired a knowledge of Latin – the key to all other learning, to a career and to advancement in it. Latin was the language of the Church and of administration, an international language which facilitated cultural interchanges throughout Europe (in the sixteenth century, Sir Philip Sidney was able to travel all over Europe, even to Hungary, conversing with scholars everywhere he went because Latin was still a common language). Virtually all the learned works in Chaucer's day were written in Latin, in the precious books, individually copied out by hand, that cost so much to buy. The boy's first introduction to Latin texts was often by way of *Aesop's Fables* – short, succinct, interesting stories with clear-cut morals to make them memorable. Next might come Ovid (43BC–AD18) – who again, especially in his *Metamorphoses*, had good stories to tell – after which parts of Virgil's (70–19BC) *Aeneid* might follow. Naturally such books often made a deep impression on their young readers, and it is not surprising that they exerted a profound and lasting influence on writers. Reading Chaucer's poems for example, we can see how often he chooses the form of the short, pithy story, easily remembered in outline, and how often allusions to classical stories occur. We may find the references to classical mythology and to ancient writers tiresome now, for often we lack the knowledge to recognise the appropriateness of the allusion, but Chaucer's contemporaries must have enjoyed being reminded of stories they also knew, or could ask to be told afterwards. In the stories of Aesop and the great works of Ovid and Virgil, readers found a distillation of experience, a truth to life which was both reassuring and highly regarded. Many other Latin authors both of the classical period and of later years were read by the learned, and Chaucer often refers to these writers. Since books were so few and so highly prized, it was natural to attach great significance to them. What had been written down and carefully preserved in such works could be relied upon; the distilled wisdom of the ages was not to be lightly set aside by the ignorant upstarts of the present day. And there was so little of it: Greek literature and learning were scarcely known, and only in Latin translation in any case. It was almost possible for one person to have studied all branches of available knowledge, and we see that Chaucer, with his knowledge of astronomy and medicine as well as of philosophy and literature, had an immensely wide range himself.

Though Chaucer was well grounded in the Latin which played such an important part in the English boy's schooling, it was not his only foreign language, for he was fluent in French from an early age. French was the language of the court to which he was attached, and French literature – courtly tales, chivalric romances, love lyrics and so forth – were popular and fashionable. It was natural that Chaucer's own writing should, in due course, be influenced by the French literature that he read, and his earliest work shows such influence very strongly indeed. The great French poets Eustache Deschamps (*b. c.*1346) and Guillaume de Machaut (*c.*1300–77) and the famous romance, the *Roman de la Rose* (*The Romance of the Rose*) which Chaucer himself translated into English, suggested to him themes, techniques, patterns and modes of approach for his own work.

When in 1372/3, and again later, Chaucer went to Italy, he must have had or acquired a knowledge of Italian. It was never as extensive as his knowledge of French, but it enabled him to read the works of Dante (1265–1321), Boccaccio (?1313–75), Petrarch (1304–74) and other writers. When he was writing *Troilus and Criseyde*, which to some extent is based on Boccaccio's *Il Filostrato*, he used a French translation of the Italian to help him read it. Throughout his life he seems to have preferred to read texts in French, the language which he would probably have used frequently in conversation, for full understanding.

Chaucer does not seem to have gone to university himself, though students from both Oxford and Cambridge figure in his tales (*The Miller's Tale* and *The Reeve's Tale*) and he clearly knew both towns and their environs. In his time, the university course – on which boys normally embarked in their early or mid-teens – consisted of a three year study (the trivium) of logic, grammar and rhetoric. Further study entailed a four year course in which the student proceeded to the quadrivium, which involved arithmetic, geometry, astronomy and music. We do not know anything about the studies of the students in *The Reeve's Tale* (except that the miller jokingly tells them that they can make a small room any size they like by the power of argument that they have learned), but Nicholas in *The Miller's Tale* is well versed in astrology, or astronomy, used to doing mathematical calculations, and skilful with musical instruments. Chaucer may, however, have gone to one of the Inns of Court, which provided further education suitable for a young man seeking a court career. His studies would mostly have been the legal sciences, but there were probably some more social activities as well, for music and dancing (useful courtly accomplishments) seem to have been included in the curriculum, which also allocated time to religious observances. Chaucer would already have had some instruction in courtly manners and etiquette, and he had also learned how to bear arms as a soldier. He does not seem, however, to have been very much interested in any aspect of military matters, and one can imagine that his participation in the war in France in 1359, which led to his being taken prisoner, was quite enough for him, and left him with less enthusiasm for chivalry than had some of his contemporaries.

Chaucer quite often mentions his love of reading: at the beginning of *The Book of the Duchess*, for example, in *The Parliament of Fowls*, and perhaps most notably in the Prologue to *The Legend of Good Women*, where he says 'On bokes for to rede I me delyte' (30). He must have been to a very large extent self-educated, devouring everything that he could lay his hands on. His works show him as not only widely read in classical and contemporary literature, but also in the sciences of astronomy, alchemy and medicine, as well as in philosophy and theology.

A further aspect of medieval education should perhaps be mentioned because of its implications for the literature of the time, and that is the necessity of relying upon memory. When textbooks – indeed books of all kinds – were so rare, people often had to learn by heart, or do without, information given to them by word of mouth. Means therefore had to be found to facilitate memorising. One device, still occasionally surviving in various forms today, was the 'places of memory'. Points to be remembered – for an argument, for example – could be associated in the mind with points in a familiar room. Then, recollection of the room with its various features would bring back the items to be remembered. Things needed to be made easily memorable if they were to lodge in the mind, and often schematic patterning assisted this: the Seven Deadly Sins, the Five Joys of Mary, the patterns of three that occur everywhere, and all the correspondences (as in the prayers in the temples in *The Knight's Tale*) and the correlations and contrasts that we find in the literature of earlier times. Chaucer does not expect his work to be enjoyed only as an aural experience, however. He speaks of *Troilus and Criseyde* as his little book; he tells a *reader* to turn over the leaf and choose another tale if unable to face the churlish Miller's tale. But although he looks forward to his work being read, it is firmly based in the tradition of oral literature, intended for a listening audience, and often incorporates some of the features characteristic of literature not freely available for private reading. We often have, for example, a strong sense of the story-teller giving us *his* version of a tale, and indeed we can discover that in subtle ways the story-teller is manipulating the response of audience or reader. Often, instead of being plunged straight into a tale, as we usually are when we open a modern novel or read a short story, Chaucer devises a transition for us from the ordinary everyday world to the imaginary world of the story, giving time for the imagination to make the journey to the long ago and far away.

Education, then, was both highly prized and difficult to obtain. At the end of his life, when Chaucer takes his leave of his readers at the end of *The Canterbury Tales*, he quotes St Paul's words: 'Al that is written is writen for oure doctrine'; and earlier, before the Pardoner begins his tale, the 'gentils gonne to crye, ". . . Telle us som moral thyng, that we may leere"' (323–5). They are eager for helpful instruction, and this has significant implications for the modern reader: there may be more to Chaucer's stories than just the narrative interest. We need to be on the alert for the 'doctrine' which Chaucer usually leaves us to discover for ourselves, if we are to appreciate the depth as well as the brilliance of his poetic powers.

Chaucer's reading

In *The Legend of Good Women* Chaucer alludes to his pleasure in reading, and the range of references to earlier authors in his works show that, despite his professional duties, he was very widely read. Though some of the texts that he mentions are rarely read today, others are still well-known, and the student of Chaucer's work may enjoy and will certainly benefit from making their acquaintance.

In Chaucer's life-time, the constant cultural interchange between England and France despite the war meant that the influence of French literature as well as of other art forms was strong. Chaucer could read French, Latin and Italian, though he found Italian more difficult. His early long poem, *The Book of the Duchess*, shows the influence of the French writers Machaut and Froissart, and of the *Roman de la Rose*. Froissart, Chaucer's contemporary, was a poet and historian, interesting for his accounts of court life in England, and of the war between England and France; while the immensely influential *Roman de la Rose* is of particular significance to all students of medieval literature. The first part of the *Roman de la Rose*, by Guillaume de Lorris, written in the middle of the thirteenth century, provided a pattern for Chaucer's dream-poems, while the second part, by Jeun de Meun, written sometime later, helped to suggest – among other things – the Pardoner's and the Wife of Bath's Prologues. Chaucer himself translated some part of the *Roman de la Rose*, and like other poets of his time, was influenced by its analysis and presentation of the experience of love.

Chaucer knew no Greek, but he was well read in Latin. He frequently drew on Ovid, whose *Metamorphoses* make enjoyable reading today. He was probably more familiar with works written in medieval Latin, than with the great classics of Latin literature. Virgil's *Aeneid* was, however, a major source for the story of Troy, though other later Latin writers contributed to Chaucer's knowledge of it. A small part of Cicero's (106–43BC) writing was also known to him including the *Somnium Scipionis* or *Dream of Scipio*. This comes from a longer work, the *De Republica* VI, which was lost in the Middle Ages but known through the Latin commentary on it written in about AD400 by Macrobius. In this commentary the *Dream of Scipio* was preserved. Chaucer refers to the *Dream of Scipio* in *The Parliament of Fowls* line 31. The commentary of Macrobius on the *Somnium Scipionis* provided Chaucer with a rich fund of material on a subject of life-long interest to him, dreams.

Perhaps the Latin work that most deeply influenced him was Boethius's *De Consolatione Philosophiae* (*The Consolation of Philosophy*). Boethius (*c.*AD480–?524) was a Roman philosopher and statesman, a friend and adviser to the Emperor Theodoric. He became a consul in 510, but later fell from favour and was brutally put to death after a long period in prison, during which he wrote *De Consolatione Philosophiae*. Though it does not make easy reading today, his great work repays study, both for itself and for its interest as a source of Chaucer's most profound thought.

Some better known Latin writers – such as Horace (65–8BC), the Roman poet who wrote a famous treaty on the art of poetry, and Juvenal (*c.*AD60–130), the great Roman satirical poet – are also referred to by him, though they made less impact upon him than did Boethius. Many of the Latin works that he read probably came to him in rather piecemeal fashion, as items in anthologies, bound up with a miscellaneous collection of other manuscripts, rather than in the form of the single complete texts that we know today.

In Italian literature, Chaucer knew Dante well, and owed much to the *Divine Comedy*, a work readily available at the present day in good modern translations. He read Petrarch (from whose Latin version he took *The Clerk's Tale*), and Boccaccio's *Teseida* and *Il Filostrato*, though he seems not to have known this author's most famous work, the *Decameron*, a collection of one hundred tales.

Chaucer had wide general interests as well as literary ones. He was very well-informed about the science of his day, and images drawn from the whole range of fourteenth-century scientific knowledge pervade his poems. Astrological references predominate, and his *Treatise on the Astrolabe* shows that he had a working knowledge of the practical aspects of judicial astrology. In *The Nun's Priest's Tale*, we get a particularly good indication of Chaucer's range of knowledge, since theories about the causes and significance of dreams, medical information, allusions to the contemporary theological debate about free-will and predestination (with its antecedents going back to St

Augustine (AD345–430) one of the greatest of early Christian writers) as well as a great many literary references, enrich the texture of the traditional story.

Chaucer and science

Chaucer makes extensive use of scientific material in his works; he seems to have had a detailed intellectual grasp of the science of his day. Though we should now consider much of it mere superstition, in the Middle Ages when men had no means of proving hypotheses and relied on the authority of ancient writers, they could not know when their theories and assumptions were false.

In the eyes of medieval men, the world they lived in had been created by God to a logically ordered design, in which each creature had its special place and function. They believed that the earth was at the very centre of the universe, and that around the earth the seven planets revolved, each in its own sphere. Out beyond the furthest was the Primum Mobile (the 'First Moevere' of *The Knight's Tale* (2987)), the force by means of which God controlled the movements of the heavenly bodies. The effect of such a world-view was thus in one way to emphasise the significance of man and of life on earth. It also underlined the belief in God's providence and in his plan for the world and for the human beings that he had created, a plan which could be seen working itself out throughout history.

According to the medieval world-view, the region between the earth and the moon was the region of air, and of generation and decay. Above the moon was the region of ether and of incorruptibility, in which the planets moved in their concentric courses. As they moved, the planets transmitted their influence to earth, affecting it in three separate ways: each planet exerted its characteristic influence upon metals, upon human beings, and upon the larger destinies of nations.

The position and movements of the planets were thought to influence the individual from the moment of birth, and throughout his life, affecting his temperament and his destiny. The horoscope, worked out from the position of the heavenly bodies at the time of birth, was thought to be a reliable indicator of character and future destiny, as we see with the Wife of Bath, who explains the blend of lustfulness and aggressiveness in her nature by pointing out that she is 'al Venerien/ In feelynge', while her heart is 'Marcien' (*The Wife of Bath's Prologue* (609–10)) – the position of Venus and of Mars at her birth was thus held responsible for her character and her behaviour.

No distinction was made between what we now think of as astronomy, and astrology. Astrology was intellectually respectable because it was linked with religion, since the movements of the planets and their consequent influence upon life on earth were thought to be under the control of God. The fact that the planets had the names of the classical deities, Mercury, Venus, Mars, Jupiter and Saturn, suited Chaucer's poetic purpose particularly well, for it meant they could figure appropriately as instruments of divine power in stories with a classical setting (such as *Troilus and Criseyde* and *The Knight's Tale*). At the same time their operations could be understood by the medieval reader as being compatible with his own religious belief.

Chaucer makes frequent reference to astrology throughout his works. By referring to the position of individual planets at crucial points in his narrative – as when he informs us of the position of the moon, Saturn and Jove (Jupiter) in *Troilus and Criseyde* (III.624–8) which produces torrential rain – he is able to emphasise the sense of the inevitability and the destined nature of what is to come. Chaucer often motivates narrative action by reference to the stars; he also makes considerable use of astronomy, in the modern sense, to indicate the time of day, as for example when the Host, in the *Introduction to The Man of Law's Tale*, deduces that it is precisely ten a.m. on the eighteenth of April, by observing the position of the sun.

In the Middle Ages, the universe in general, the macrocosm, was thought to correspond to man in particular, the microcosm. Just as on earth there were the four elements of fire, air, water and earth, made up of the four contraries of hot and cold, moist and dry, so in the human body there were four contraries which made up the four humours. The concept originally came from Hippocrates, who taught that good health depended upon the maintenance of a balance between the four humours in the human body. The humours were choler, or yellow bile, which was produced by a mixture of hot and dry; sanguine, in which blood predominated, produced by a blend of hot and moist; melancholy, or black bile, resulting from a mixture of cold and dry; and phlegm which came from a mixture of cold and moist. The medieval doctor not only had to calculate the astrological influences which might affect the patient whom he was treating, but he had to endeavour to correct the balance of the humours when they got out of proportion. Chaucer's Doctor in the *General Prologue* to *The Canterbury Tales* is well 'grounded in astronomye' (line 414) which enables him to work out the best time for treatment. He also knows 'the cause of everich maladye/Were it of hoot, or coold, or moyste, or drye' (419–20), and so is able to prescribe appropriately.

Chaucer shows a knowledge of some other aspects of medieval medicine in *The Nun's Priest's Tale*. He lists medical authorities; and Chauntecleer's wife, Pertelote, displays some expertise on the subject of medicines for a disordered stomach. Though to a modern reader they may seem more suitable for farmyard fowls than for human beings, these remedies were in fact accepted in contemporary medical practice, or had been recommended by authorities in the past. Though much medieval medicine depended more on superstition than on science, some herbal lore has remained valid to the present day.

The concept of the four humours usefully helped to categorise types of person: Chaucer's Reeve in the *General Prologue* is a 'sclendre colerik man' (587) quick to anger, while the Franklin is 'sanguine' and therefore cheerful and hearty. Physiognomy, the study of facial characteristics, was also believed to be a reliable indicator of the character, as also of the moral condition of the individual. Chaucer makes use of this branch of science, or pseudo-science, in the portait of the Summoner, whose revolting appearance and complexion marred by skin disease is an indication of the sinister traits suggested by other details that Chaucer gives us.

Magic may also be mentioned here, because 'magyk natureel', such as that practised by the Doctor in the *General Prologue*, was regarded as a form of science in Chaucer's time. Those who practised it used a special knowledge of natural phenomena, such as the position of the planets. When, in *The Franklin's Tale*, the Clerk of Orleans gets to work with his Toledan tables to calculate when the tide will conceal the rocks for longer than usual, we are told 'It semed that alle the rokkes were aweye' (1296). We see that the magic of the clerk seems to consist rather more in his knowledge of astronomy than in any special powers. The disappearance of the rocks appears to be illusory rather than actual. Such 'magyk natureel' is to be distinguished from the black magic which involved conjuring up evil spirits, and which was strictly forbidden by the Church.

Finally, dreams may be included in this brief survey, since Chaucer's writing reveals his abiding interest in them. There was controversy as to the extent of their significance, as the argument between Troilus and Pandarus in *Troilus and Criseyde* (V.316–85) makes plain: Troilus is sure that his dreadful dream about Criseyde in the arms of a hideous wild boar is a reliable portent (as indeed it turns out to be), while Pandarus is sceptical. Chaucer drew much of his information on the subject from the commentary of Macrobius on the *Somnium Scipionis* of Cicero. Macrobius categorised dreams as belonging to five main types. The first, the *somnium*, was a dream foretelling the future, but (as with Troilus's dream) needing to be interpreted because it was of an allegorical nature. The *visio* gave a pre-vision of future events, exactly as they were to happen; while the *oraculum* was a dream in which a venerable person appeared and revealed things that afterwards came true. These three types of dream were thought to result from the reason remaining awake while the body slept. Macrobius also defined two other types of dream, resulting from the activity of the imagination working during bodily sleep without the aid of reason. These were the *insomnium*, a dream of wish-fulfillment or of waking preoccupations; and the *visum*, characterised by meaningless, fearful phantasms experienced between sleep and waking.

Chauntecleer refers to Macrobius in *The Nun's Priest's Tale* in his learned discussion of the significance of dreams with his sceptical wife, Dame Pertelote; he insists that they are to be heeded as warnings, while she insists that his dream is merely the result of bodily indisposition. Though the theories by means of which medieval men endeavoured to explain the origins and meaning of dreams can no longer be accepted, modern psychology suggests that dreams may often have a real significance in revealing what is going on in the unconscious mind of the dreamer, information which he may be neglecting at his peril.

Part 2

Chaucer's works

Chaucer's early poems

The Book of the Duchess

One of Chaucer's earliest poems, *The Book of the Duchess*, was written (probably in 1369) shortly after the death from plague of Blanche, the first wife of John of Gaunt, Duke of Lancaster. It is a formal poem of consolation for the bereaved husband, and a memorial of the charming young Duchess. In writing it, Chaucer was much influenced by and borrowed much from the French poets, in particular Guillaume de Machaut, with whom he was familiar. Like many other contemporary writers, Chaucer was attracted to the form of the dream-poem and chose it for *The Book of the Duchess*: it enabled him to treat his royal patron's bereavement with delicacy and tact and a certain indirectness, without seeming to intrude. It was not for Chaucer, the young poet, to recommend resignation or to offer religious consolation to the Duke of Lancaster; instead he found a subtle way of celebrating the loveliness and life of Blanche, so soon cut short, and her husband's happy love for her.

Chaucer takes us into a dream-world in which he encounters a grief-stricken young man in black, who eventually begins to tell the cause of his sorrow. Fortune, he says, has played a game of chess with him, and taken his queen. The dreamer is mystified, and encourages the man in black, a knight, to tell him more. He describes how when very young he had come to fall in love with a ravishingly beautiful lady. At first she rejected him; but at last he won her, and she gave her love to him. In dwelling on his past life he conjures up the perfections of his beloved lady and the whole complex experience of falling in love, crowned at last by the supreme happiness of possessing her in marriage. The dreamer asks where she is now and the question forces the knight to return abruptly to the present, as he answers 'She ys ded', confronting once more the loss that he had forgotten in his evocation of his love. Thus the poem creates a living image of Blanche and a sense of how she was prized by her husband, ending with the shocked confrontation of her death and his loss.

Chaucer takes us gradually into the dream-world of the poem. He begins by speaking of his own problems, of his inability to sleep and of how he took a book to 'drive the night away', in which he read the story of Ceyx and Halcyon, told by Ovid in his *Metamorphoses*. When King Ceyx was drowned, his wife died of grief, but not before she was granted a dream in which the gods allowed her dead husband to bid her farewell. Reading this sends the poet to sleep, and his own dream begins, in which he wakes in a room in a castle when he hears birds singing on a May morning, and a horn blowing for a hunt. He goes out and soon finds himself in the wood, where he encounters the man in black.

The beginning of the poem leads into its real subject by introducing the theme of loss: a queen mourns a king, providing an image later mirrored (rather than paralleled) by the lover's grief for his lady's death. The reader (or audience) is led deeper and deeper by gradual stages into the dream-world in which the sorrowing knight, indirectly representing John of Gaunt, mourns his loss and speaks of his love. The beauty of the setting distances and softens the tragic experience, as the morning sun shines through the jewel-bright stained-glass windows of the castle, and a royal hunting party rides past, pursuing a hart, as later the knight in black will 'hunt' his dear heart, 'goode faire white' (Blanche). The man in black's description of his lady presents her as surpassingly lovely, dancing, singing, laughing and speaking in a friendly way – it is a portrait that comes to life, despite the conventional terms in which she is described. At last she becomes for him 'My suffisaunce, my lust my lyf' (1038) – his whole heart's desire and source of earthly happiness – as he learns to love more deeply. Here Chaucer shows us 'courtly love' at its most courtly and charming, finding its natural fulfilment in marriage. By means of the colloquial interchanges between dreamer and knight, as well as by stylised description and song (1175–80), and the recollected words of the lover to his lady, we learn of the whole progress of their love. The dreamer's questions sometimes seem extraordinary to the modern reader: why does he not realise that the lady is dead? But his eager, sympathetic enquiries build up tension as they draw out the truth from the bereaved lover, until the final terrible fact is dramatically revealed: 'She ys ded!' (1309). No comfort can be offered; Chaucer preaches no message of spiritual consolation. Instead, the dream ends, and he takes us back to the beginning, to the book and the story that he was reading before he fell asleep.

In *The Book of the Duchess* we have a conventional medieval dream-poem, but a poem full of feeling, both passionate and delicate, and full of brilliant detail. Chaucer writes in rhyming couplets, in octosyllabics – that is to say in short, four-stressed lines, a rather restricting form – but the dialogue in particular adds dramatic touches to the poem. By taking part as dreamer in the action, he transforms what might have been a static eulogy into something much more dynamic. The 'Chaucer' he presents to us is a 'persona' suited to his purpose: unhappy and troubled, deferential and rather imperceptive, a figure that cannot be literally equated with the 'real' Chaucer, but rather the kind of figure that the poem requires. Early work though it is, Chaucer's ingenious blend of convention and originality makes it a moving and lovely elegy.

The House of Fame

The House of Fame is also in the form of a French love vision, written in octosyllabic couplets, but long though it is, it is unfinished. In the Proem, Chaucer discusses the topic of dreams, which interested him all his life, before beginning the story of how, on 10 December, he fell asleep and dreamed that he was in a temple of glass. On the walls of the temple was written the story of the *Aeneid*, from which Chaucer tells the sad history of Dido, seduced and deserted by Aeneas. The temple is the temple of Venus, who is here seen as representing sexual love in its unhappy as well as its pleasurable aspects; and Chaucer's verses are rich with allusions to other betrayed women in classical mythology.

When the dreamer leaves the temple, he sees a great, shining golden eagle alighting and in Book II, he is carried aloft in its claws to new discoveries. The eagle explains that he has been sent by Jupiter to reward 'Geffrey' for his service to Cupid and Venus, mentioning how the poet sits up reading far into the night after his day's work, and living almost like a hermit. He is to be taken to the House of Fame, to hear news of love and of 'Loves folk'. As they travel on, the eagle gives Chaucer a lecture on the properties of sound, and tries to instruct him about the stars, despite his protest that he is too old to learn. Then the House of Fame is reached and Book III begins. The dreamer sees first a huge, melting rock of ice, on which are engraved the names of the famous, and then the House of Fame itself. The great writers of the past are there, but the dreamer sees how arbitrarily Fame treats new arrivals, some with favour, while some get only slander. Eventually he is asked why he has come, and whether he is seeking fame too. His reply repudiates the idea that he wishes for public recognition: 'I wot myself best how y stonde' (1878), he says. But he then explains that he has come to learn some new tidings, some new things 'of love, or suche thynges glade' (1889). He is next rather inexplicably conducted to the House of Rumour, made all of twigs, and constantly whirling round. As it is full of holes, so it lets out a great sound, to Geffrey's amazement. The eagle is at hand to explain that Jupiter intends him to be consoled for his distress by learning some new things here, but before they can be revealed, there is a great noise in one corner of the hall. It seems that news of love is being discussed, but before the dreamer can discover what is going on, a man of great authority appears – and the poem ends.

The House of Fame is both an entertaining and a very learned poem, yet the overall effect is bewildering. Though it is a dream-poem, Chaucer breaks away from convention in rejecting the usual garden setting; and though, as often in such poems, the dreamer has a guide, the eagle is a most unusual one. Though there is much that is didactic, the teaching that the dreamer receives is general rather than moral; and the way in which it is given and received is often amusing rather than solemn. The poem both achieves a dreamlike quality and gives a sense of actual experience, as 'Geffrey' is constantly presented with new and unexpected sights and sounds. But exactly what it is that he hopes to learn is never made clear; and in fact he never does hear the news that he so eagerly seeks. Though *The House of Fame* is in many ways a delightful poem, it fails to satisfy the reader, partly because it is unstructured and partly because no clear-cut meanings emerge.

The Parliament of Fowls

In this early work Chaucer again uses the form of the dream-poem, this time to give expression to some of his thoughts about love. He explains at the beginning that, though love is such a wonderful thing, he knows of it only from books, and not from first-hand experience. While reading one of his books, *The Dream of Scipio* by Cicero (Marcus Tullius) (see page 35), he fell asleep and had a marvellous dream in which he was guided by Scipio's ancestor (Africanus) into a garden, then to the Temple of Venus, and then to a grassy place where all the birds had met, on St Valentine's day (14 February) to choose their mates. First to choose were three eagles, who all wished to have as their mate the same young female eagle, a formel, but the other birds – in particular the goose, the duck and the cuckoo – became very impatient at the delay that ensued. The eagles' love for the formel was such that they could not agree to set it aside – as the lesser birds would have done – and choose another mate, and in the end the goddess Nature, who was presiding over the occasion, agreed to postpone the decision for a year so that the lesser birds could choose their mates. When this was done, the birds sang a happy song in honour of St Valentine, and the dreamer awoke.

The poem divides into three parts, of which the first contains Chaucer's general comments on the great experience of love, and on *The Dream of Scipio*. He describes how Scipio asked his ancestor in his dream to tell him how he could enter into the bliss of heaven, and was told that he must first realise that he was immortal and then must work for the common good of mankind, out of love for his fellow men. After this kind of love has been mentioned, Chaucer falls asleep and dreams that Scipio Africanus becomes his guide. In the second part of the poem, thus guided, the dreamer encounters a very different kind of love when he passes through a gate into a park, for the gate leads to the bitter-sweet experience which awaits the servants of Love – among whom the dreamer, a mere observer, is not numbered. In a beautiful garden, he sees Cupid, the god of love, and his daughter, Wille, or sexual desire, and many other figures, all personifications of different aspects of the experience of love, dancing round a temple. Inside it, he sees first Priapus, representing the most crudely carnal aspect of love, and then the voluptuous figure of the goddess Venus reclining naked on a golden bed. Perhaps unexpectedly, everything here suggests the suffering that may result from the indulgence of the most sensual aspects of love, as well as the pleasure. It is a very different kind of love from that advocated by Scipio Africanus to his descendant, yet it too is called love.

Then the third part of the poem begins, as the dreamer moves out into the garden again, where Nature has gathered all the birds together, and where yet other kinds of love are to be presented. The goddess holds on her wrist a beautiful young formel eagle, and the three male eagles who seek her as their mate offer her their loving and lifelong service and devotion and ask for her mercy and grace. Their speeches take so long that the other birds become impatient and begin to quack and squawk and complain, until Nature tells them to be quiet. The goose suggests that the lovers rejected by the formel eagle should find other mates, but the turtle-dove recognises the absurdity and impropriety of the idea: 'God forbede a lovere shulde chaunge!' (582). The formel eagle is allowed to choose for herself and she asks for a year's respite. Nature grants the request, tells the lovers to continue to serve their beloved and gives all the other birds their mates. It becomes clear that this part of the poem is not about the ways of nature, but about kinds of love – that of the noble nature, contrasted with the ordinary person's simple desire to mate. The vulgar mind and coarser nature (represented by such birds as the goose and cuckoo and duck) cannot begin to understand the faithful, unchanging devotion of the nobler spirit. Chaucer thus shows that love is experienced in very different ways, and can take very different forms, but even at its noblest, it may bring with it serious problems. What is the rejected lover to do, since he loves with a true passion that can never change? If his love could cease or change, it would not be true love; thus he may be left in an intolerable position.

The poem, while it presents many different aspects of love from the most altruistic to the most grossly carnal, reaches no conclusions. As so often with Chaucer, we are left to ponder on the complexity of human experience, and the problems with which it confronts us.

Chaucer uses a five-stressed line in a seven-line stanza, a unit that allows him some flexibility, as the poet drifts into sleep and moves from one strange sight to another in his dream. The poem is rich with imagery as the poet recounts his experiences, blending personification and classical allusion with sensuous perceptions. Sound and sight, the senses of touch and of smell lend it vividness, while a delightful humour enters the poem when the vulgar birds assert themselves. In passages of lively dialogue Chaucer shows the contrasting attitudes of the various birds, not without touches of social satire. The poem also belongs to the medieval genre of the love-debate, in which problems concerning love were considered, but its richness, variety and depth make it much more than a conventional treatment of the theme of love.

Chaucer's prose works

Boece

A work which exerted a powerful and lasting influence on Chaucer was *The Consolation of Philosophy* by the sixth-century Roman, Boethius, and he translated it from Latin into English prose (*c.*1380). *The Consolation* tells of how Boethius, in prison, deprived of all his wordly goods and honours, and in danger of death, is visited by a woman of 'ful greet reverence', the Lady Philosophy. His discourse with her brings comfort in his misery, as she enables him to come to a clearer understanding of the purpose of human life and the relationship of the earthly to the divine, so that he can ultimately accept his misfortune.

Though the work is not overtly Christian, it is based on the premise that God, who made the world, is good, and that true happiness is only to be found in Him. Boethius deals with the problem of evil in the world: since God cannot do evil, evil is nothing, arising out of the wicked passions of men. God is reality, and therefore evil cannot be real. The Lady Philosophy explains how by turning away from the changing, perishable pleasures of this world – the riches, honours and other earthly satisfactions that by their very nature cannot last – and searching for the 'verray blisfulnesse that is set in sovereyn God', the sorrows of this world will fade into insignificance. Her teaching depends on the proposition that mind is superior to matter: 'The mind is its own place, and in itself/Can make a heaven of hell, a hell of heaven,' as John Milton (1608–74) says in *Paradise Lost*, Book I. Such a belief must have been particularly congenial in an age when the privations of life were severe and suffering often so irremediable. The Lady Philosophy explains that in this world all things are bound together in harmony and controlled by the operation of love: 'al this accordaunce of thynges is bounde with love, that governeth erthe and see'. Love binds the hearts of men together in fellowship. We see how important these ideas were for Chaucer in, for example, Duke Theseus's speech at the end of *The Knight's Tale*, and *Troilus and Criseyde* (the Invocation, Book III).

The Consolation of Philosophy also deals with a problem which vexed Chaucer's contemporaries: do human beings have free-will, or are they predestined by God to suffer and act as they do? The Lady Philosophy explains to Boethius that contrary to what may seem to be the case, men do have free-will, but that God sees what choices they will make. For God is in eternity, outside time, and past, present and future are all one to Him. Thus He sees what choices human beings are going to make, but leaves them free to make them. Troilus in Book IV of *Troilus and Criseyde* wrestles with this problem, but unenlightened by philosophy, he never reaches a clear understanding, and concludes miserably 'Thus to ben lorn [lost], it is my destinee' (IV.958–9).

Chaucer's translation of Boethius's *Consolation* is not very easy to read, but even a brief study of this great work is rewarding both for itself, and for the increased understanding that it gives of Chaucer's thought.

A Treatise on the Astrolabe

For a little boy, Lowys or Lewis, probably his own son, Chaucer wrote a small book on how to use the astrolabe, an instrument used for calculating the positions of the heavenly bodies. Chaucer's knowledge of astrology and astronomy was considerable, and he very frequently refers to astrology in his other works. He considered a knowledge of the astral bodies and their movements an important part of education. Much of the treatise is translated from Latin sources, and it has been thought to be the oldest work written in English on an elaborate scientific instrument. Perhaps the most striking feature of this work for the modern reader is Chaucer's sympathetic understanding in writing in English to make the task easier for 'Lowys', 'for that curious endityng and hard sentence is ful hevy at onys for such a child to lerne.'

Troilus and Criseyde

The story

In *Troilus and Criseyde*, Chaucer tells the story of Prince Troilus, one of the younger sons of Priam, King of Troy, and of his love for Criseyde, the widowed daughter of the traitor Calchas, who went over to the Greeks when they were besieging the city. It is a story of passionate love, set against a background of war. Troilus is a very young man when the story begins, quite inexperienced in the ways of love, so that when he sees the beautiful young widow Criseyde and falls irresistibly in love with her, he does not even know how to begin to make her acquaintance. His great friend Pandarus, however, is Criseyde's uncle, and when at last he discovers what is upsetting Troilus, he gets to work to bring about a meeting. Eventually Criseyde is persuaded to look kindly upon Troilus, but they can very seldom see each other, for Criseyde insists that no-one should know of Troilus's love for her, so that her reputation will not be endangered. Troilus's love increases more and more and eventually Pandarus, in pity for him, contrives a private meeting with Criseyde. He gets her to come to supper at his house one evening when he knows that there will be torrential rain, because of which she is forced to stay the night. Pandarus persuades her to receive Troilus in her bedroom, on the pretext that Troilus has heard a rumour that she has shown favour to another man and is dying of grief. Criseyde weeps at the idea that Troilus should suspect her of any such thing, Troilus faints when he sees his beloved's tears, and Pandarus puts him into Criseyde's bed to revive him. Eventually, they consummate their love and for a time their mutual happiness is very great.

Then news comes that there is to be an exchange of prisoners of war: Criseyde is to be sent to join her father in the Greek camp, while the Trojan Antenor returns to Troy. Troilus cannot ask King Priam for Criseyde's hand in marriage, for she is the daughter of a traitor – not a suitable match. Criseyde will not let him simply carry her off somewhere – she insists that she will get back to Troy quite easily within a few days. So Troilus has to let her go, against his better judgment.

In the Greek camp, she is lonely and friendless and at once Diomede, also a king's son, begins to force his attentions upon her. She very soon gives way and becomes Diomede's mistress, while Troilus, heartbroken, waits despairingly for her to keep her promise and return. At last he realises that she is completely unfaithful; and eventually he is killed in battle. Looking down on this world after death, he sees how trivial are the joys of earthly life compared with the joys of heaven.

The sources

The story of Troilus and Criseyde is an episode (as is Shakespeare's (1564–1616) play *Troilus and Cressida*) in the ancient story of the Trojan war, the subject of Homer's epic, the *Iliad*. When the Trojan Paris carried off Helen, the wife of the Greek Menelaus, the Greeks besieged Troy for many years, until at last they were able to capture and destroy it by means of the great wooden horse, filled with Greek warriors, that the Trojans unwittingly dragged into their city. The story of the fall of Troy is told by Virgil in the *Aeneid*; it was a story of special interest to medieval Englishmen because it was believed that the British were originally descended from the Trojans.

Chaucer found the story of Troilus in Boccaccio's poem, *Il Filostrato*, written in Italian about 1330 (though Chaucer used a French translation of the poem to help him). A version of the story had been told before by the French poet Benoît de Ste Maure in the twelfth century in his *Roman de Troie*, and this work was in turn based on two short Latin works, the *De Excidio Troiae* by Dares (*c.* AD 600) and the *Ephemeridos Belli Troiani* by Dictys Cretensis (*c.* fourth century) both briefly referred to by Chaucer in his poem. Twice in *Troilus and Criseyde*, Chaucer mentions the source of his information about his characters as being a certain Lollius. In fact no such writer ever existed, but Chaucer seems to have shared a general belief, arising out of a misunderstanding of one of the verse *Letters* of the Latin poet Horace, that Lollius was an earlier authority on the Trojan war.

Though Chaucer followed Boccaccio's story quite closely, he gave his poem a new meaning, bringing to it a philosophical depth that it did not have before, and enriching it in many ways.

The opening of the poem

In the very first line of the poem Chaucer indicates the outline of the story. He is going to tell us of the 'double sorwe' of Troilus: in his love for Criseyde and then in his loss of her. It is to be a tragic story, and Chaucer invokes Tisiphone (one of the three Furies of classical mythology) to help him tell it. Thus the poet builds up an appropriate atmosphere before beginning his story, taking his audience or readers gradually into the world of the story, and appealing to the young lovers among them for their sympathetic understanding; he does this in language that has a solemn, even a religious tone. It is only at line 57 that he actually begins his tale, setting the scene by referring to the well-known background of the Trojan war.

Chaucer as storyteller

In the opening stanzas of the poem we are made aware of the poet, preparing us for what is to come in the story as a whole before he begins to tell it. Throughout the poem, however, he continues to remind us of his presence as he directs our attention and makes general comments or evaluations, as well as telling us what is actually happening. At first he assumes the guise of a mere 'servant of Love's servants', too unworthy to be a lover himself. He often closely involves his audience or readers by such remarks as 'This, trowe I, knoweth all this compaignye' (1450), making himself seem less knowledgeable than they. So he projects a personality for himself which immediately enriches the poem, by giving us the impression that we are in the hands, not of an omniscient narrator, but of someone who is responding with sympathy and enthusiasm to the experiences of the characters and their changing fortunes, just as we are. Our sense of listening to the true story of real people is heightened at some points when Chaucer says that he cannot tell us more, because he does not know himself – for example, whether Criseyde had children or not, and whether she really believed that Troilus was out of town when she agreed to dine at Pandarus's house. By this means, he involves us more completely by suggesting and making us ponder various possibilities.

Towards the end of the story, Chaucer creates an extraordinary effect of distancing his characters, as events draw to their intolerably sad conclusion. Criseyde seems immensely far away, psychologically as well as spatially, in the Greek camp. We no longer have any sense of contact with her, or of what is going on in her mind. To achieve this effect, Chaucer gives little formal descriptions of Diomede, Criseyde and Troilus (V.799–840) which make them seem as if they were complete strangers retreating into the distance.

At the very end, when the story of Troilus is concluded, Chaucer brings us back from the imaginary world of Troy to the everyday world and sets the lives and actual experience of his audience or readers in the context of eternity and of spiritual reality, ending his poem with a prayer for the future.

The main characters

In the course of this long poem we feel that we come to know the characters very well, to understand and to sympathise with their motives, as we often do when reading more recent works of fiction. Yet we must resist the temptation to regard *Troilus and Criseyde* as 'the first modern novel', if we are to gain a true understanding of a great medieval masterpiece. For the characters despite their lifelike appearance, are representative figures, who act as they do because that is what their story necessitates, rather than individuals set in motion by their author. Through them, however, Chaucer communicates the deeper meanings that the story implies. Though the characters are types, through Chaucer's subtle story-telling we do come to know Troilus, Criseyde and Pandarus well.

Troilus is very young when he first appears, the leader of a group of 'yonge knyghtes', but not yet a lover: indeed, he laughs at and despises lovers. When he falls in love, he suffers agonies of helpless despair before he can be persuaded to tell Pandarus the cause of his distress. Chaucer represents his torments with a sympathetic humour; Troilus's swooning and weeping are slightly ridiculous, even if indicative of an admirable depth of feeling. But there is nothing absurd about the selfless devotion and faithfulness into which his first boyish infatuation develops. Chaucer makes Troilus the very embodiment of trustworthiness and integrity, and his behaviour is always consistent with his dominant characteristic: he cannot go against his nature, for example, by disregarding Criseyde's wishes when the news comes that she is to be exchanged for Antenor; his lack of sexual aggressiveness is prompted by his fear of distressing Criseyde by forcing his attentions upon her; and what seems like weakness when he is incapacitated by love is offset by his courage in battle.

Criseyde is Chaucer's most enchanting heroine; but while Troilus's love for her is unshakeable in its faithfulness, her love for him is less deeply rooted. It is her nature to be changeable, but also to be timid, anxious and insecure. When the story opens, Criseyde, widowed and abandoned by her father, and consequently unprotected, is terrified of the Greeks. She is also beset by fears of losing her good reputation and of making her position more precarious by being known to have a lover. In the Greek camp, bereft of the 'wal of stiel' (III.479–80) that Troilus has been to her, she soon succumbs to Diomede when he offers to love and care for her. But Criseyde is a very positive character, too: socially at ease in the highest society; poised but also playful; volatile, but capable of obstinacy – for example, when she refuses to hear of any other course of action than compliance with the order to leave Troy. Chaucer shows us a woman with affection and spirit, but very little understanding of the political situation and the realities of war.

Pandarus is little older than his niece Criseyde or his friend Troilus – himself a lover, but an unsuccessful one, it seems. He is sympathetic to Troilus's suffering and fond of his niece, but incapable of understanding Troilus's finer and deeper feelings. He delights in manipulating circumstances and people, in fixing things up to give maximum satisfaction to all parties. Without him the lovers would never have come together, but he has conscience enough to have qualms about arranging, in effect, for Criseyde's seduction. His intentions are always of the best, however, and as Troilus is not only his close friend but his feudal overlord, he feels bound to do what he can to promote his happiness.

Diomede is the most slightly-drawn character, but he provides an admirable foil to Troilus. He knows what he wants and no moral scruples or fear of giving offence hinder him from forcing his attentions on Criseyde. Though he, too, is a king's son, he has to point out to Criseyde that he is 'As gentil man' as any man in Troy (V.931). His odiously affected manner, his playing on Criseyde's fearfulness and his boasting of his parentage add to our sense of the contrast between him and Troilus.

Chaucer brings his characters to life mainly through dialogue and action. We come to know them through what they say and do, through what other characters say about them, and through what Chaucer tells us about them himself. Chaucer skilfully varies the way in which his characters speak. Pandarus, the practical man, has a strong proverbial element in his speech, suggesting the everyday world of affairs in which he is professionally and socially involved. He often makes learned references as well. Troilus, by contrast, is usually serious and dignified, though he several times vents his feelings in lyrical utterances (for example, the 'Canticus Troili' of I.400–20). Though the interpolation of songs is not in modern terms a realistic way of indicating an emotional character, here Chaucer effectively suggests heightened feeling and the difference of personality between Troilus and his friend. The interchanges between the characters are particularly revealing in suggesting relationships as well as personalities. Troilus's irritation with Pandarus when the latter tries to get him to tell him the cause of his suffering (I.750–6) indicates the intimacy of the two young men, despite Troilus's higher social position. Later, Chaucer shows us Troilus at his first meeting with Criseyde at the house of Deiphebus, losing all presence of mind and completely forgetting his carefully prepared speech. His character is often revealed in soliloquy, and in the desperate, insistent questioning when he confronts the torment of separation from Criseyde (IV.288–322 and V.218–45). When we see Pandarus and Criseyde together in Book II, we notice Pandarus's ability to manipulate his niece, but also her changing feelings as she moves from disappointment to curiosity and then to a half-serious mood of caution. What other characters say about Criseyde also adds to our knowledge of her personality: she is highly praised by her fellow dinner-party guests – Helen of Troy, Hector and others – after she has left (III.211–17).

What Chaucer actually tells us himself about his characters is, however, of particular significance, firstly because it often enables us to see what is going on in their minds, and secondly because it frequently makes us pause and review our assumptions about a character, so that our conception becomes more complex and subtle. For example, we see Criseyde after she has been told of Troilus's love for her, and has watched him ride past her window, considering whether to give him her love (II.656–812). Chaucer reveals Criseyde's changing moods and entire mental processes as she evaluates her situation, comes to a decision, and finally happily gets up and goes off to amuse herself. Elsewhere, he sometimes indicates what is going on in the unconscious minds of his characters by means of symbolic dreams (for example, II.925–31). He also sows doubts in the mind of the reader by declaring that he does not know what his character's thoughts were: the source, Chaucer says, does not explain what Criseyde thought when Pandarus invited her to dinner, saying that Troilus was out of town (the implication is that perhaps she suspected that he was still about and accepted the invitation, knowing that it might lead to a secret meeting).

At such points Chaucer's uncertainty makes the characters appear more life-like because he does not claim to know everything about them.

The setting

The setting of *Troilus and Criseyde* is at the same time ancient Troy and fourteenth-century London. Chaucer makes his characters behave like his own contemporaries, in a world which in many ways closely resembles his own. The love with which Troilus is so suddenly stricken affects him as it affected many another medieval lover, and causes him to bear himself well in battle, like the Squire in the *General Prologue* to *The Canterbury Tales*, 'In hope to stonden in his lady grace' (line 88). Chaucer represents the war between Greeks and Trojans as a typically medieval affair (and he had had personal experience himself of war in France) in which champions encounter each other in individual hand-to-hand combats and skirmishes outside the besieged city. Meanwhile, social life continues in the ordinary way, against a background of palaces and gardens with dinner parties and dancing, the telling of stories and singing of songs, until the final disaster, outside the scope of the poem. But the war is not going well for the Trojans, and Calchas the soothsayer predicts the ultimate fate of Troy (IV.76–7), a prediction reaffirmed later (V.883–96) by the terrifying words of Diomede to Criseyde. Thus doom hangs over the beleaguered city, and over the lives of the lovers from the beginning. Criseyde longs for news that the siege is ended: when we first see her with Pandarus she says 'I am of Grekes so fered that I deye' (II.124). Troilus and Criseyde are finally caught up in the complex military and political situation that forms the background to their lives: parliament decides that Criseyde must be exchanged for Antenor, and at once the issues involved become too complex for there to be any way out for Criseyde.

At the same time as Chaucer gives us a sense of what war was like in the Middle Ages, and of courtly life, he ingeniously suggests a classical background appropriate to the tale of Troy. He was aware that in such remote times, many aspects of life must have been different – an unusually acute perception for a medieval writer – when he says 'Ye knowe ek that in forme of speche is chaunge/Withinne a thousand yeer . . . (II.22–3). Modes of love-making must have been different, too, he suggests. He gives the poem a distinctly classical atmosphere by his many allusions to the classical gods. Jove, Venus and Mars play a part in the fortunes of his characters, particularly Venus; and references to Apollo, as well as the invocations at the beginning of each book – to the Muse Clio, to Tisiphone and the other Furies and to the angry Fates – give a classical tone to the poem. Troilus visits the shrine of Apollo and prays to Venus. He tries to understand why such misery should fall upon him and as a pagan he decides that it is 'necessity', rather than Providence, that has brought it about. When Troilus at last dies, it is Mercury who comes to take him to his appropriate place. But in the last stanzas, Chaucer returns us to 'present' – fourteenth-century – time, and to an explicitly Christian world-view, rejecting the pagan gods, 'Jove, Apollo, . . . Mars' and 'swich rascaille' (V.1853), who can offer no comfort to suffering humanity.

Destiny, fate and fortune

In *Troilus and Criseyde*, Chaucer uses the word 'destiny' and a word of similar meaning, 'wyrdes', to suggest the pattern of the individual human life, which, though full of ups and downs, was, for the medieval Christian, ultimately under the guidance of God. Chaucer only uses the word 'fate' three times; he never uses it to suggest the hostile, indifferent or impersonal power that we often associate with fate now.

Troilus, living in the pre-Christian era, could not share the medieval belief in the loving providence which shaped each man's destiny for his ultimate good. In his soliloquy in the temple in Book IV, he comes to the conclusion that it is inevitable that he will be 'lorn' or lost, 'For al that comth, comth by necessitee' (IV.958); he has been predestined to suffer, he believes, and has no free-will. Chaucer gave greater philosophical depth to his poem, particularly at this stage in the story, by drawing upon *The Consolation of Philosophy* written by Boethius while awaiting death in prison in the sixth century. In this work Boethius ponders the problem of whether we have free-will, or whether all that befalls us in life is predestined to do so, so that we cannot escape our fate. In his trouble, a lady 'of ful greet reverence' comes to him, the Lady Philosophy, and answers his questions. In *Troilus and Criseyde*, though the questions that Troilus asks are similar to those of Boethius, he can find no consolatory answers. He remains convinced that Fortune is his enemy, and that there is no way in which he can avoid the suffering that she brings him.

In *The Consolation*, Philosophy explains to Boethius that Fortune brings about all the short-lived pleasures of this world as well as worldly misfortunes. Riches, power, fame and success in love are the gifts of Fortune. All such gifts are necessarily transitory and so can bring no lasting happiness. Only by turning away from worldly ambitions and the love of earthly things, and by devoting himself to the love of God can a man avoid the sadness of losing prized earthly blessings. So, in this great work, Boethius asserts that the mind can be free: free to reject and to transcend the ephemeral pleasures of this world and to choose the lasting satisfactions of the spiritual one. Thus, though God has foreseen all that is going to happen, man still has free-will, freedom of choice, within the overall pattern of his destiny. God, in His eternal present, outside time, sees past, present and future, and sees what choices each human being will make, while leaving him free to make them.

Troilus of course knew nothing of all this, for he lived in the ancient world of pagan deities and directed his prayers to Venus. Only after his death, when he looks down upon 'This litel spot of erthe' (V.1815) and is able to despise 'This wrecched world' and see its vanity in comparison with 'the pleyn felicite/That is in hevene above', does he understand what the Lady Philosophy had explained to Boethius. Shortly after this, in the final stanzas of the poem, Chaucer urges the young members of his audience to turn away from worldly vanity themselves, and give their hearts to God, who will never fail them. The implication is that they can deliberately choose, because they are aware that they have a choice; Troilus did not realise that he had any alternative but to love Criseyde.

For Chaucer and his contemporaries, human destinies were influenced by the movements of the planets. Venus had been in a favourable position at the moment of Troilus's birth (II.680–3), and so exerted a beneficent influence on his later life. Though it was thought that the horoscope cast at birth could reliably predict events in a person's life, it was possible to believe that a person was not completely at the mercy of the stars. The response, for good or ill, to the events the stars foretold was still within man's conscious control.

Astrology and mythology

Chaucer was able to assimilate pagan deities such as Venus into a poem with a Christian framework, because the planets were named after them. Each planet, according to medieval belief, exerted an influence on human beings and their affairs, under God's ultimate control. In the poem we see that Pandarus is an expert in astrology, and thus able to predict the exceptional weather that will make it impossible for Criseyde to leave his house after the supper party. Chaucer's own knowledge of astrology was quite extensive, and throughout his work he makes reference to the positions of the heavenly bodies to indicate times and seasons. In Book III of *Troilus and Criseyde*, for example (1417–20), the position of the morning star indicates that the lovers must part.

Just as Venus can be both the pagan goddess and the planet, so she can also be 'Joves doughter deere' (III.3), the beloved daughter of Jove, or Jupiter, and so a vehicle for the love of God. 'Jove' may thus refer to the planet Jupiter, or to the god of classical mythology, but may also indicate the God of Christianity. At the very end of the poem, however (V.1849–55), Chaucer denounces Jove, Apollo and Mars and other pagan deities, for their service can bring no everlasting happiness or heavenly reward, and he prays to the Trinity, and especially to Jesus, for protection.

Tragedy

Chaucer describes his poem as a little tragedy (V.1786) but in what sense is it a tragedy? Medieval literary theory defined tragedy as a fall from high to low, brought about by Fortune, and ending with death. Tragedy befalls those who have valued highly the gifts of Fortune, such as riches, and worldly success, which cannot last to all eternity; but such tragedy can be avoided if we choose instead to lay up for ourselves treasure in heaven so that death implies not loss, but gain.

To Troilus, his own tragedy seemed to be the tragedy of necessity, not of choice, for he was unaware, as a pagan, that he could have acted other than as he did. He did not know that he could have set his heart on heavenly things, and so avoided earthly loss.

The medieval tragedy of Fortune is thus unlike classical tragedy, in which the hero is the helpless victim of a hostile fate; and unlike Shakespearean tragedy, in which a fatal flaw in the hero causes him to act in a way which ultimately brings about his downfall.

The ending

The ending of *Troilus and Criseyde* has puzzled many people, because in it Chaucer seems to reject the love which throughout this long poem, he has represented as life's most enriching and wonderful experience. When the story of Troilus and Criseyde is finally concluded, Chaucer turns to his audience or readers, and advises young people, for whom it is natural to fall in love as Troilus did, to turn away from the 'worldly vanity' of earthly love, the 'feynede loves' of this world, and love God, who will never betray them, as Criseyde had betrayed Troilus. It is a counsel of perfection – logically, the only way to avoid the sorrow that Troilus endured, and to be sure of everlasting life after death. Because we are human beings, subject to the limitations of our mortal nature, we cannot have it both ways, but we do have a choice. In this unexpected epilogue to the story of Troilus, Chaucer recognises the complexity of our lives, and the paradox that the experience that yields the most exquisite happiness may also bring the deepest sorrow.

Love, honour and 'trouthe'

Again and again in his poetry Chaucer returns to the topic of love, and in *Troilus and Criseyde* he represents the experience of love as one of the most intense and ennobling that a young man can have. It is all-absorbing; and when fulfilled, energises and gives to the lover a new dynamism. Deprived of its joy, Troilus finds that life is not worth living. At the present day love may still be as exciting, but in its medieval manifestations it was rather different from love in the twentieth century. Such instantaneous falling in love was part of a long established literary convention, represented by the visual image of Cupid with his bow (though in the fourteenth century Cupid was seen not as a chubby infant but as a young man). The effects of Troilus's experience in the temple when he first sees Criseyde are striking: he takes to his bed in great distress, unwilling to admit even to his best friend, what is the matter with him. At last he is persuaded to reveal his secret; secrecy matters, for naturally he does not want his private affairs to be gossiped about. Every medieval lover, moreover, knew that if he was to obtain his lady's favour, secrecy was essential. But one trustworthy confidante was permissible, and Troilus could never have become Criseyde's lover in the fullest sense of the word without Pandarus's help. He was too shy and inexperienced and reluctant to force his attentions upon Criseyde.

The relationship between lovers was not seen, as often at the present day, as a kind of intensified, heightened friendship between equals, but very much more as a feudal relationship. The expectation was that the lover would serve his lady. Troilus actually offers to do this (III.141–7), hoping Criseyde will look upon him with favour, if she accepts his service as from a position of superiority. The lover in his humility hoped that his lady would show mercy – be kind – and that he would win grace from her. In the course of time, she might grant him her love, and marriage would follow. Of course the lover's real desire was to possess his lady: marriage was the means by which such possession was made socially acceptable, and legally secure. Troilus, as we see, eventually achieved the happiness of possessing Criseyde; but not being married to her, he had no security.

Not all lovers conformed to these conventions in exactly the same way. Troilus, young, shy and inexperienced, behaves very differently from the brash, forceful Diomede, who loses no time in furthering his own interests with Criseyde. The lover was expected to be able to plead his cause eloquently: 'Kan he wel speke of love?' (II.503) asks Criseyde of Pandarus, when he has been telling her about Troilus. But Troilus, when the moment comes for him to speak, finds that all his carefully prepared words of love vanish from his mind, and the brave young soldier prince can only choke out 'Mercy, mercy, swete herte!' to his beloved (III.98).

The lover was expected to be obedient to his lady's wishes. It seems strange to the modern reader that Troilus, when brought to Criseyde's bed by Pandarus on the night of the 'smoky reyn' merely faints away when the situation seems to call for action. But Troilus loves Criseyde so intensely that he cannot bear the sight of her tears, cannot even think of doing anything to displease her. If he had acted differently, he would not have been Troilus. But then, as now, very deep feelings expressed themselves through the physical symptoms of weeping or fainting. We never see Diomede overcome by strong emotion, for obvious reasons.

If marriage was the ambition of the medieval lover, why did Troilus and Criseyde not marry? Criseyde was the daughter of a traitor (as Ector mentions in I.117) and so would not have been considered a suitable bride for the king's son, who would have been expected to make an appropriate political match. When she has to be exchanged for Antenor, Troilus cannot ask his father to intervene, since to do so would reveal that he and she were already lovers (IV.554–60), and it would have been unthinkable to ask King Priam to reverse his decree. Before the proposal for the exchange of prisoners it would not have seemed worthwhile to raise the question of marriage and to risk the king's anger. Indeed, following the events so skilfully arranged by Pandarus, Troilus's longing had been satisfied and Criseyde's reputation was unblemished. It would not even have seemed necessary for them to marry.

The modern reader may still remain puzzled as to why Troilus did not follow his better judgment and carry Criseyde off somewhere, out of Troy, to avoid the exchange of prisoners. The answer is that she did not want him to because she feared for her reputation and believed that she could get back; and loving her as he did, he could not go against her will.

When, in Book III, their love has been consummated, Troilus expresses his deepest feelings about love, in a passage closely based on *The Consolation of Philosophy*, in which Boethius says that it is the bond of love that holds married couples together. Troilus cannot *assume* that Criseyde and he will be thus securely joined, but he prays that love will 'bind their agreement', as in the case of married people it should do: 'Love, that of erthe and se hath governaunce . . . Bynd this acord, that I have told and telle' (III.1744–50). His splendid lyrical appeal to the cosmic force of love celebrates and praises its power over married couples, over the nations, even over the four elements and over sun and moon, sea and land. Chaucer shows the love of Troilus and Criseyde as a relationship of deep mutual devotion and mutual trust. It is a love which is spiritually as well as physically fulfilling, ending tragically because of the adverse external circumstances which separate the lovers. Though Criseyde fails Troilus, he cannot find it in his heart 'To unloven [her] a quarter of a day!' (V.1697–8), so unshakeable is his devotion to her, even when he knows the whole extent of her unfaithfulness.

In *Troilus and Criseyde*, the concept of love cannot be separated from the ideas of honour and 'trouthe'. From the beginning, Criseyde is shown to be anxious about her honour. In every way she is a timid, fearful young woman, afraid because after her father's defection she is unprotected, afraid of the Greeks, but most of all, afraid of losing her honour. For a woman, honour consisted in preserving her reputation for chastity; her dread was, as we see with Criseyde, that she might be talked about, be known to be having an affair. Criseyde only consents to have anything to do with Troilus on condition that absolute secrecy is preserved, and her honour safeguarded (for example in II.468; 479–81; 760–3). She loses no honour when Troilus becomes her lover, for the discreet Pandarus alone knows about it. For a man, however, honour consisted in his reputation for courage, military prowess, and loyalty, and Troilus is highly honoured in these respects. When Criseyde is to be exchanged for Antenor and Troilus suggests that he and she should 'stele away' (IV.1503), she rejects the idea, not only on the grounds that her reputation would be destroyed (IV.1576–82), but also because Troilus's honour would be lost (IV.1574–5), since he would be accused of lustfulness and, worse still, cowardice.

Throughout the poem, it is Troilus's 'trouthe' that is his dominant characteristic. To the very end, he is true to Criseyde, and to his own nature in being so. It is his 'trouthe' that made Criseyde love him, as she says in IV.1667–73 – his absolute trustworthiness and unshakeable faithfulness. This quality of integrity, which Chaucer was later to make the key to the meaning of *The Franklin's Tale*, involved much more than merely telling the truth: God is truth, and in possessing this quality, human beings in a sense, share in the divine nature, which cannot change. Criseyde's 'trouthe', however, was not deeply rooted. She was, as Chaucer says, 'slydynge of corage' (V.825), unstable. In deserting Troilus, she destroyed her own honour and her 'trouthe', as Troilus poignantly has to acknowledge at the end: 'O lady myn, Criseyde, Where is youre feith . . . where is youre trouthe? . . . Who shal now trowe on any othes mo? . . . Allas, youre name of trouthe Is now fordon, and that is al my routhe' (V.1674–87). Criseyde's treachery destroys all trust, invalidates every oath, while Troilus's unchanging love remains unworldly, impractical perhaps, but noble in its strength and patience.

Structure

Troilus and Criseyde begins, like many poems of its time, with an introductory passage which prepares the audience or reader for what is to come, and allows the poet to build up an appropriate atmosphere, before he launches into his story. At the end, Chaucer gradually returns his audience or reader from the imaginary world of Troy and its inhabitants, to the world of everyday experience, ending with a short prayer. Thus the story is presented within a functional framing device.

Each book begins with an appropriate invocation (except for the last where there are brief references to classical mythology instead) which sets the tone for what is to follow, whether sad or joyous. Each book has its own divisions into separate scenes as the story progresses and the characters interact with each other, or their mental processes lead them into new situations. Each scene represents the characters' state of mind at a particular moment; and the transitions are often made explicit by the poet's comments as he creates a pause in the story which allows him to comment or evaluate.

The concept of Fortune also helps to shape the poem, for Troilus's life follows the inexorable course of Fortune's wheel. He rises from prostrating sorrow to the height of bliss, and then falls lower and lower into misery, until finally death claims him. He progresses 'Fro wo to wele, and after out of joie', as Chaucer tells us in the first stanza of the poem.

Chaucer followed Boccaccio's story in *Il Filostrato* quite closely, but he expanded it at various points, extending the account of Troilus's wooing of Criseyde and adding to the philosophical depth of the poem in various ways. The five books into which the poem is divided allow for a very symmetrical patterning, as the long awaited happiness of Book III gives place to the sorrow that ends the story somewhat as it had begun. In the prologue to Book IV, however, Chaucer seems to suggest that it was his intention to complete the poem in four books. Presumably he later found that he could not conclude it satisfactorily without allowing himself more space, particularly if, as has been thought, Troilus's soliloquy on free-will and predestination was not included in his first draft but was a later addition.

Style

Chaucer used rhyme royal for *Troilus and Criseyde*, a form which he had used before in *The Parliament of Fowls*. This form consists of a seven-line stanza with an iambic line of five stresses, which allowed him to create a very varied range of effects, from solemn invocation to naturalistic passages of dialogue. Chaucer's command of tone allowed him, furthermore, to alternate passionate or tragic emotion with lively comedy, as the story demanded: and to rise from vivid descriptions of the practical transactions of everyday life to lyrical utterances of the most elevated and stylised kind.

An examination of some features of the first book of *Troilus and Criseyde* will illustrate the great range of effects that Chaucer creates within the rigid stanzaic form of the poem. He begins with a compressed outline of the story and a solemn invocation in epic style, but with an appeal to the audience that makes use of liturgical language (reminiscent of church services) to build up a solemn atmosphere. Only after this does he turn to his real subject, simply sketching the situation in Troy at the beginning of the story. Soon, however, we learn of Troilus's sensations as, in love for the first time, he expresses them through the stylised medium of a formal song. In a subsequent passage of soliloquy Troilus's disturbing new emotions are expressed through exclamatory and questioning outbursts, while Chaucer makes us feel that his unrestrained behaviour is at the same time pathetic and absurd. When Pandarus insists on knowing what is the matter with Troilus, the naturalistic dialogue suggests the impatient irritability of the sleepless, suffering youth (see, for example, I.1622–3).

Pandarus's frequent use of proverbial expressions not only creates the impression of a practical, down-to-earth character, but is used by Chaucer for dramatic effect by contrast. An example of this occurs when Troilus, before being brought to Criseyde's bedside in Book III, prays to Venus for grace and inspiration in words which create a feeling of devotion, while Pandarus in exasperation exclaims 'Thow wrecched mouses herte,/Artow agast so that she wol the bite?' (III. 736–7). At this point we are made keenly aware of two markedly differing attitudes to the situation: Troilus's spirituality and feeling of insufficiency and awe, as opposed to Pandarus's insensitivity and very physical attitude to love.

Chaucer achieves a variety of effects through the sparing use of metaphor and symbol. Particularly through natural imagery, he succeeds in suggesting mood and feeling, or turning points in the story. When Criseyde, after deciding that she will accept Troilus's love, hears as she lies in bed a nightingale singing in the garden (II. 918–19), its song makes her 'herte fressh and gay', and when she falls asleep, the bird-imagery continues with symbolic force as she dreams that an eagle takes her heart out and replaces it with his own. Later, Chaucer describes Criseyde as being like a hapless lark in the claws of a sparrow hawk as she quakes with fear (III. 1191–2), but soon she is to be like the nightingale – the bird of love – as, reassured, she 'Opned hire herte' to Troilus.

Throughout the poem, Chaucer's use of dialogue brings the characters to life; and humour often breaks in, even at serious moments, so that we can better realise the complexity of experience. Chaucer suggests that even the most serious love affair may have its funny side. He holds the readers' interest by frequent use of such contrast and by changes of tone, as much as by creating moments of suspense in the narrative.

The Legend of Good Women

In about 1386, soon after writing *The Knight's Tale*, Chaucer wrote once again on the loss and betrayal of love, the subject of his earlier great work, *Troilus and Criseyde*. *The Legend of Good Women* consists of a series of poems about betrayed women, based on the poems of Ovid. The subject was inevitably a limited one and Chaucer seems to have wearied of it before the intended series of poems was completed. It also appears that this work did not spring from any strong urge on Chaucer's part to tell tales of this kind, but that he was asked to write it to make amends for his having written of women unfaithful in love. Not only had he told the story of Criseyde's unfaithfulness to Troilus, but he had translated what might be considered a misogynistic poem, *The Romance of the Rose*. Though in *The Legend of Good Women*, it is the God of Love and his queen, Alceste, who reproach Chaucer and make the request in the Prologue to the poem, it seems probable that Richard II's young queen, Anne of Bohemia, is thus indirectly referred to as having set the subject for the poet.

About ten years after Chaucer composed the first version of the Prologue, he revised it, and both drafts have survived (referred to as Text F and Text G, as in Robinson's edition of the poet's works). Each version includes a list of the poems that Chaucer had written, the Text G is updated to include some later works.

In the Prologue, Chaucer speaks of his delight in reading, which is second only to his delight in walking in the fields in May, when the daisies are in flower, and he wishes that he had the ability to praise this much-loved flower adequately, in 'ryme or prose'. He asks lovers to help him, whether they are 'with the leef or with the flour', a comment which makes a rather obscure allusion to parties at court. Characteristically Chaucer does not take sides with either. Then he describes how, after wandering in the meadows, he eventually falls asleep and dreams that he hears birds singing on a delightful morning in early summer. The God of Love appears, a beautiful young man, with his queen Alceste, and a company of ladies who sing a 'balade'. The God of Love reproaches Chaucer for so boldly appearing in his presence, since he has dared to commit offences against the law of love by writing of faithless women. Alceste defends Chaucer, who pleads that he had only intended to further and foster truth in love, and she sets him the task of writing of faithful women. In Text F, the book, when completed, is to be given to the queen 'at Eltham or at Sheene' (line 497), the palaces of Richard II. (In Text G, Chaucer removed these lines, for Queen Anne had died in 1394, and Richard in his grief had had her palace destroyed.) When he wakes, the poet begins the task with the story of Cleopatra.

Chaucer seems to have abandoned the work just before completing the ninth in what was to have been a series of nineteen stories of good women. In a sense, they provided a bridge between his earlier and his later work, for the idea of the collection of stories was to be developed much more effectively later in *The Canterbury Tales*. Inevitably, all the accounts of good women were bound to turn out somewhat alike – in form, in tone, and in point of view. They could not allow Chaucer the range that his genius needed, and which he achieved in *The Canterbury Tales* by having a variety of narrators telling their very different tales. In

The Legend of Good Women the stories of Cleopatra, Thisbe, Dido, Hipsipyle and Medea (both betrayed by Jason), of Lucrece, Ariadne, Philomena, Phyllis and Hypermnestra are told somewhat in the manner of medieval saints' lives, though Chaucer sometimes ends a tale with a rather flippant comment. Such exemplary heroines by their very nature could not have the human interest or offer such scope to the writer as the characters of the Wife of Bath, Alison in *The Miller's Tale*, Dorigen in *The Franklin's Tale* or May in *The Merchant's Tale*. Their classical origins and the necessity of telling their sad stories in courtly style imposed further restrictions on Chaucer.

Chaucer used the decasyllabic couplet for the first time in English in *The Legend of Good Women*. He was later able to exploit the form to full effect in many of *The Canterbury Tales*.

THE CANTERBURY TALES

Though *The Canterbury Tales* are still widely read and studied, it is often as individual works rather than as a whole. Yet Chaucer conceived of his masterpiece as a totality in which tales of many different kinds, told by storytellers of many different kinds, could contrast with and complement each other. From the 1380s on, Chaucer had a number of stories and poems that he wanted to gather together. He also had the idea of grouping them by inventing characters to tell them. Since, however, the stories were very miscellaneous, he needed a miscellaneous group to tell them, and the best example of such a group in the fourteenth century was the pilgrimage. Such a social occasion could naturally bring together a very varied collection of people with a serious common purpose, but whose mood might well have been lighthearted, as they set aside their everyday preoccupations for a short time. As people from many different walks of life, they would naturally tell very different tales; pilgrims, in any case, were known to be great storytellers.

When Chaucer had described the pilgrims, he arranged the stories in groups for variety, in such a way that one story could relate to another. After the pilgrims had drawn lots for the first storyteller, Chaucer put the Knight's story, written some years before, first. Then *The Miller's Tale*, concerned with a love triangle of a different kind, could appropriately follow; but since *The Miller's Tale* mocked a carpenter, Chaucer followed it with *The Reeve's Tale* to allow the Reeve, also a carpenter, to get his revenge. As he was unsure how to continue, he started *The Cook's Tale*, but soon gave it up, and so the first section of *The Canterbury Tales*, known as Fragment 1, comes to an end.

Other stories also fall into groups in which stories are contrasted or complement each other. When Chaucer died, he must have left a cluster of manuscripts in which the stories existed in groups, probably not yet properly related to each other; and since he was still working on them, there were internal inconsistencies, in the references to the time of day and the point on the road reached by the pilgrims. He also changed his mind with regard to the number of tales each pilgrim should tell.

After his death, some unknown editor put the stories into a possible order, since it was certain that the *General Prologue*, followed by *The Knight's Tale*, began the sequence, and that *The Parson's Tale* ended it. Within this sequence it is possible to discern ten distinct fragments. The order found in this most famous, early manuscript, the Ellesmere, has been followed by Robinson in his edition (to which reference is made throughout this book). Although there are inconsistencies because Chaucer never made a final revision, we may as well accept the order of the tales as it is found in Ellesmere.

A number of *The Canterbury Tales* touch on various aspects of marriage. This is perhaps not surprising, since there are a number of comic tales and married couples are a traditional topic for popular comedy. Some critics, however, have thought that this indicates a thematic treatment by Chaucer (the so-called 'Marriage Group' of tales), and it certainly reflects one of his characteristic interests; but there is nothing systematic about it. This group of tales is, for example, interrupted by the Friar's and the Summoner's tales, which have nothing to do with marriage. Chaucer was always interested in personal relationships, just as he was always interested in religion and in comedy, and it is natural that such topics should crop up frequently.

So, though Chaucer did not live to complete his scheme, for each of the thirty pilgrims was originally intended to tell two stories on the way to Canterbury and two on the way back, he nevertheless did produce, not a random collection of stories, but tales which often relate to each other significantly. Furthermore, he introduced in the *General Prologue* a fascinating collection of characters; and in the links between the tales, he showed these people talking and often clashing with each other in very naturalistic and spontaneous dialogue. He could also suggest audience-reaction, particularly in the comments of the Host, as master of ceremonies.

General Prologue to *The Canterbury Tales*

In the *General Prologue*, we see the company of pilgrims meeting together at the Tabard Inn in Southwark for the journey to Canterbury. Chaucer probably lived in Greenwich, on the pilgrimage route, from 1385 to almost the end of his life, so that he would have seen pilgrims assembling and setting off in just this way. The journey to Canterbury usually took about three days, though it could be done in less. The shrine of St Thomas, who had been murdered in 1170 and canonised three years later, was a major place of pilgrimage, and must have been a splendid sight in Chaucer's time, adorned as it was with great quantities of gold and jewels.

The poem opens with a passage about spring, the season when people long to get out and about after the rigours of winter. Such a passage was a conventional literary device, often used to set the scene in a medieval poem, but here Chaucer's genius goes far beyond the traditional set piece. He gives us not only a quintessential sense of the season itself, but a vivid realisation of its stirring effects on human beings. Soft rain and warm breezes, freshness and fragrance, new growth and the song of birds help to make up the picture of England in April; and the new life in nature finds its counterpart in a human longing for change and for new experience.

The Canterbury Pilgrims

At the end of the *General Prologue*, Chaucer says that he has described the 'estate' of all the pilgrims; his prologue is thus not merely a collection of portraits, but something that goes much further. In the Middle Ages what is now known as 'estates satire' was popular: literature that described the characteristic qualities and failings of the members of the various 'estates', the trades, professions and ways of life of fourteenth-century people. Thus, in describing the pilgrims, Chaucer was not inventing a galaxy of interesting characters, or portraying actual people that he knew, but drawing upon a well-established but rather stereotyped mode of writing and transforming it by his genius, to give us the highly individualised group of people who make up the company assembled at the Tabard Inn. At the same time that he indicates the common failings attributed to the social group to which each belongs, he makes us believe that each one is a unique individual. His method of doing this is a very subtle one, for we often have to read between the lines to realise that Chaucer is criticising the pilgrims at all: the Monk, for example, is a 'manly man', the Pardoner 'a noble ecclesiaste', assertions which we may take at face value until we realise how pervasive Chaucer's irony is.

In order to give a more comprehensive view of his society, Chaucer presents a very large company of pilgrims, and selects representatives from high up on the social scale (the Knight and his son, the Squire), and from both religious and secular life. He has women as well as men, he has poor as well as rich, learned and ignorant, and simple countrymen as well as sophisticated, worldly pilgrims. The **Knight**, given first place, represents the highest class, though Chaucer has not taken, as he might have done, a powerful nobleman. Though most of the other pilgrims are satirised, Chaucer's Knight is presented as an entirely admirable member of his class, a representative of chivalry. Chaucer five times mentions his 'worthynesse', his nobility; and he is also wise, unassuming and unostentatious. It seems likely that Chaucer intended to associate him with the crusaders: he fights for a religious ideal rather than for personal aggrandisement and has participated in many campaigns in foreign countries. His 'array', described at the end of the portrait, suggests an unworldly disregard of outward appearance combined with concern for professional competence. As the pilgrimage begins and the tales are told, the Knight's social superiority and moral authority are recognised by the rest of the company including the Host.

The **Squire**, the Knight's son, is also a representative of chivalry, but he is above all a young lover, as is natural for his age, and his devotion to his lady inspires him to perform deeds of valour. The Squire, unlike his ascetic father, does not scorn elegant clothes or disregard his appearance: he is the embodiment of the romantic ideal of the young lover, with all the accomplishments that were considered appropriate. He is accompanied by a Yeoman whose admirable professionalism and practical ability qualifies him to be the servant of both Knight and Squire.

Next in the assembly of pilgrims comes the **Prioress**, Madame Eglentyne, whom Chaucer describes in terms of a worldly beauty, as if she were the heroine of a romance rather than a woman dedicated to a life of religious devotion. Earlier writers had satirised women, including nuns, as being sensual and fond of luxury, caring more for their pets than for the sufferings of the poor: Chaucer makes his Prioress a beautiful and charming woman whose courtesy is her dominant characteristic. We do not know whether the brooch which she wears, on which is inscribed 'Love conquers all things' (162), refers to the love of God, or to earthly love, but it allows Chaucer to suggest that the values of the Prioress are worldly rather than spiritual. She is the feminine counterpart of the Squire, for whom courtesy is also a dominant characteristic; but we are left with an uneasy feeling that the virtue of courtesy that is perfectly appropriate to him, is somehow not quite what the Prioress should be making her prime aim.

Following the Prioress comes the **Monk**. Monks were often satirised, particularly for the gluttony and lack of spirituality traditionally attributed to the monastic orders. Chaucer subtly suggests that his Monk is fond of good food, but he does not explicitly state that he is greedy: he makes the Monk appear physically attractive: 'a fair prelaat;/He was not pale as a forpyned goost' (204-5), rather than as gross and bloated. He is fond of fine clothes and loves hunting, but Chaucer leaves us with a sense that perhaps we should approve tastes so natural, and which produce such attractive results, rather than condemning them as unsuitable to the Monk's vocation. We know that it is wrong for the Monk to prefer the sound of his bridle bells to the sound of church bells, but we can sympathise, because Chaucer makes us accept the Monk's own point of view instead of that of the conventional critic. In the end, we both condemn the Monk for not living up to the spiritual ideals that we suspect he should uphold, and approve of him as an attractive and very human individual.

In Chaucer's time friars were subject to at least as much censure as monks, for they, too, frequently failed to live up to the ideals to which they were dedicated. They were particularly criticised for their over-persuasive speech and flattery, often leading to the seduction of women. Like the Monk, Chaucer's **Friar** is an attractive figure, with his pleasant speech, healthy appearance and musical ability, but he has disagreeable characteristics, too. He is greedy for money, extorting it even from poor widows by his fair speech. Like the Squire, the Friar is 'Curteis . . . and lowely of servyse' (250), but only when it is to his financial advantage ('ther as profit sholde arise' (249)). Though much of the time we can read the traditional criticism of friars between the lines, and contrast with it the Friar's own opinion of himself, we are also made aware of a third viewpoint, for Chaucer reminds us that the Friar is consciously making his own self-assertive estimate of himself ('For he hadde power of confessioun,/As seyde hymselfe, moore than a curat' (218–19)). Like the Monk, the Friar does not live up to the ideals of his order, and as with the Monk, we are made aware of the tension between the spiritual ideals and the expectations of the everyday world in which he moves, of which he – in a sense naturally – accepts the standards and values.

Next comes the **Merchant**, who of course belongs to the secular rather than to the ecclesiastical world. Merchants were traditionally associated with fraud and dishonesty and Chaucer's choice of words such as 'chevyssaunce' (dealing in money (282)) implies that his Merchant's dealings were probably shady ones. The very respectable and dignified appearance that the Merchant maintains probably both masks dishonest money-operations and enables him to conceal any losses that he may make, which might undermine the confidence of his clients: 'Ther wiste no wight that he was in dette' (280), because he makes sure that no-one knows if he is in debt. As with his other characters, Chaucer allows us to approve of this pilgrim by concealing his faults from us and letting him present his reassuring public image. Though we may suspect that the appearance does not entirely coincide with the reality, Chaucer bars us from registering disapproval by giving us no sense of the victims of the Merchant's malpractices. Whereas with some characters (the Friar, the Pardoner and the Summoner, for example) the victims of exploitation are indicated, with the Merchant there is no suggestion that any individuals are the worse for his financial transactions.

Unlike the Merchant, the **Clerk** (or scholar) is to be regarded as an admirable figure. He does not seem as attractive as many of the other pilgrims, with his half-starved appearance, bony old horse and threadbare clothes. He cares nothing for worldly success, and he spends no time trying to make money; unlike such pilgrims as the Friar, he does not waste words, though he finds time to pray for the souls of any who will enable him to further his studies. His devotion to scholarship and his readiness to pass his learning on would have been dear to Chaucer's own heart (for in *The Legend of Good Women* and elsewhere, Chaucer indicates his own delight in books), and they also conform to the contemporary ideal for the scholar. It was accepted that such a person should be unworldly, and though by the standards of the Prioress, the Monk and the Friar, the Clerk's indifference to wealth and the pleasures it can bring seems extraordinary, and by the ordinary standards of social behaviour he is plainly a dry old stick, his single-mindedness is to be heartily approved. Though he is not self-indulgent he is not mean, for he is willing to share with others – gladly – what is most precious to him.

The **Sergeant of the Law** is not equally admirable, for like the Merchant, one of his dominant traits is the exploitation of other people for his own advantage. He is a well-to-do, self-important lawyer, who has made money by buying land, as the term 'fee symple' (319) indicates, and Chaucer hints in the line 'Of fees and robes hadde he many oon' (317) that perhaps they have come to him as bribes, rather than being fairly earned. His character is summed up in the lines 'Nowher so bisy a man as he ther nas, And yet he seemed bisier than he was' (321–2), which indicates that he puts on a show of being in great demand for his professional expertise; but as with the Merchant, we have to take him at his own valuation, and are not shown how the victims of his self-enriching activities feel about him.

The **Franklin** who comes next is also a well-to-do landowner, a man who takes delight in food but who offers hospitality generously. His complexion, we are told, is 'sangwyn' (333), suggesting an attractively fresh, rosy appearance – Chaucer's contemporaries believed that in each human being, one of four humours predominated, making them phlegmatic, melancholic, choleric or, as in this case, sanguine, and of a cheerful disposition. He is a country gentleman who has held responsible positions, and although he is not presented as an ideal figure like the Knight or, later, the Parson, there seems to be no suggestion that he is not to be regarded with approval.

The next pilgrims arrive in a group – the Haberdasher, Carpenter, Weaver, Dyer and Tapicer (tapestry-maker) – and although their trades are different, they all belong to the same social and religious guild, and thus to the same social level. They are ambitious, successful, worldly citizens, on whose class the economy must have depended to a large extent – four of them are concerned with the important cloth trade – but Chaucer has nothing special to say about them, and they never get a chance to tell their stories in the course of *The Canterbury Tales*. We do not even hear details of their individual professional activities as we do with the other pilgrims, unlike the **Cook** who follows them, a very skilled exponent of his trade. However, our growing interest in his culinary gifts is checked by reading of his most unpleasant defect, the disgusting ulcer on his shin which, mentioned in close conjunction with a list of the food that he prepares, gives us second thoughts about his suitability for his profession.

The **Shipman**, or sailor, is described in terms of the characteristics traditionally attributed to his calling, to which Chaucer adds the little significant details that make the pilgrims seem so life-like. Sailors were notorious for their ruthless and lawless ways, and this one is typically without conscience, given to stealing and even murder ('By water he sente hem hoom to every lond' (400)). Not for nothing does he wear a dagger hung round his neck, half-concealed under his arm. Certainly he is experienced and expert at his craft with his knowledge of tides and harbours, but a dangerous man, even though he too is on a religious pilgrimage.

The **Doctor**, who comes next, is unique too, but Chaucer's phrase, 'He was a verray parfit praktisour' (422), invites comparison with the first pilgrim to whom we were introduced. Like the Sergeant of the Law, the Doctor is a professional man who can impress his hearers with the apparently vast extent of his knowledge, which includes astronomy (or astrology, as we should call it) and 'natural magic'. So much in demand is he as a doctor that he is very well-to-do, but our uncertainty about whether he is to be approved of as obviously a very good doctor, or disapproved of as enriching himself by other people's suffering, remains unresolved. His arrangement with apothecaries for the dispensing of medicines enriches all concerned, but is evidently very efficient; his lack of study of the Bible may make him seem indifferent to religion, but on the other hand, he may simply be too busy attending to the sick. Times of plague add to his wealth, but then he risks his life by attending the infected. We are, however, left with the firm impression that if we were to meet the Doctor, we would be much impressed by him.

We could not fail to be impressed by the **Wife of Bath**, either, were we able to meet her, though rather by her enormous vitality and dominant personality than by the dignity displayed by the Doctor. As with the other pilgrims, this portrait is also based on traditional literature, in this case misogynistic satire which discussed women's faults and failings and the appropriate attitudes towards them that men should adopt. Such writing often denounced women for pride and bad temper – here we see that the Wife is infuriated if she is not allowed to make her offering in church before other women. Chaucer also drew on an earlier tradition which portrayed elderly women as knowing all about love, and ready to instruct others, even when they were themselves too old for it. Here, he shows his originality by making the Wife a very experienced older woman but one who is still all too ready for love if anyone will give her a chance. Many of the vivid touches of visual detail which bring her before us as a unique person have symbolic significance, yet they do not detract from our sense of her individuality.

The **Parson** and the **Ploughman** come together: they are brothers, and both are also ideal representatives of their kind, rather than the reverse. We learn nothing of the Parson's outward appearance, but much of what he does and what he believes. He is holy, learned, patient and generous and he looks after his parishioners with the utmost care for their spiritual well-being, visiting them when they are in trouble without regard for his own convenience, and not lacking the courage to reprove them if they fall into sin, even if they are his social superiors. In creating this ideal portrait, Chaucer suggests, by contrast, the characteristic shortcomings of the clergy of his day, and at the same time indicates how a parish priest should perform his duties. His parson, unlike the other ecclesiastical figures (for example, the Monk and the Friar) seems to show that, difficult though it may be, it is not impossible for human beings to live up to the ideals to which they aspire. The Ploughman is equally virtuous, loving God and his fellow men, and being ready to work without charge to help any poor neighbour if it lies in his power. He is, it seems, skilful and energetic, but his admirable qualities leave him rather an uncolourful figure. It is significant, however, that Chaucer chose a ploughman to represent the lowest social level among the pilgrims, for his contemporary William Langland in his great allegorical poem *Piers Plowman* makes the ploughman not only the pillar of fourteenth-century society but also a Christlike figure. Society was fundamentally dependent on the ploughman for the provision of food, so that Chaucer's Ploughman may also be seen as a key figure rather than as a mere farm labourer. He and his brother the Parson, however, are separated from the other pilgrims by their ideal nature and their close relationship, and it seems probable that Chaucer, in presenting them in this way, is indicating his recognition of the need for a basis of mutual consideration and unselfish service for the benefit of the wider community, instead of the ruthless greed and self-seeking apparent in most of its members.

The **Miller** is a very different kind of person. The description that Chaucer gives, of an overpoweringly coarse, brutal and ugly figure makes a marked contrast with those immediately preceding it. He concentrates on the very physical and visual details that would immediately strike an observer – the heavy build, red beard, hairy wart, and large nostrils and mouth – which make the Miller a repulsive and potentially threatening figure. Like several of his fellow pilgrims he is also well practised in dishonest dealing: 'Wel koude he stelen corn and tollen thries' (562).

Next to the Miller is the **Manciple**, a servant whose work it was to buy food and other goods for a college or one of the inns of court, the legal institutions with which Chaucer may himself have been at one time connected. The masters for whom he works are learned men, clever lawyers, and the Manciple seems to be chiefly distinguished by his ability to serve them efficiently and well. It is possible that he enriches himself at the same time, for Chaucer tells us that he 'sette hir aller cappe' (586), or outwits them all, but he remains a shadowy figure of whom we know little but that he seems to have been – at least in his own eyes – professionally competent.

The Manciple, at this point, separates the **Reeve** from the Miller. The Miller and Reeve later turn out to be deeply hostile to each other. Whereas the Miller is immensely strong, thick-set and brawny, the Reeve is thin and seems physically weak, but he is so clever and has such a firm grasp of everthing that is going on, that many people are afraid of him. He has been trained as a carpenter (a fact which the Miller takes advantage of later in telling his own tale, in which he angers the Reeve by showing an elderly carpenter fooled and humiliated), but now he works as a farm-manager for a lord in Norfolk. His expert knowledge and efficiency allow him to give his lord satisfaction, while at the same time he has enriched himself. No one can catch him out or get away with any dishonest tricks themselves; he does not need the rusty sword he carries, armed as he is with the weapon of ruthless cunning and quick intelligence. We gain a strong impression of his personality through Chaucer's description of his unattractive physical appearance, and of his values through what we learn of the way in which he goes about his work. We are also shown something of the environment in which he works as with many of the other pilgrims: granary and dairy, seed and grain, sheep, cows, pigs, horses and poultry are under his control. We see his pleasant house shaded by trees, his fine horse and good clothes, and the ample supply of money safely stored away.

The last two pilgrims to be introduced, the Summoner and the Pardoner, are even less attractive than the Miller and the Reeve, and they also constitute a related pair. The **Summoner** was an official attached to an ecclesiastical court, whose job it was to bring people accused of various misdemeanours before the court. Summoners were hated as oppressors of the poor, all the more because they could be bribed by the more affluent to overlook their offences, and because they were themselves often guilty of the very deeds, often sexual offences, of which they brought accusations against others. The Summoner is introduced as physically repulsive, his face disfigured with a hideous and incurable skin-disease, as his moral nature is by his lecherous behaviour. We even seem to smell the pungent food – onions, garlic and leeks – of which he is so fond, foods which were traditionally associated with moral corruption. He is also given to excessive wine drinking. When drunk, he speaks in Latin, but he can only keep repeating parrot-fashion, without real understanding, the few phrases that he has heard in court. Chaucer tells us about the Summoner's readiness to accept bribes; and how he encourages those who are able to pay to defy the accusations of arch deacons – who were also often the subjects of similar satire on grounds of corruption. The Summoner is well aware the archdeacons are subject to such criticism, for he says, 'Purs is the ercedekenes helle' (658), recognising that they punish wrong-doers not by putting them in danger of hell-fire by excommunicating them from the life of the church, but by extorting large sums of money from them instead. Thus he teaches people to disregard the spiritual authority of the archdeacons; even worse, he corrupts young people, insinuating himself into their confidence and making himself their adviser.

In this portrait, Chaucer instead of appearing to applaud the attitude of this subject as he does, for example, with the Monk ('And I seyde his opinion was good' (183)) disagrees at one point with the Summoner's assertions when he comments, 'But wel I woot he lyed right in dede' (639). However, despite this and the repellent impression that is created overall, we are still encouraged to take the Summoner on his own valuation too. He sees himself as 'a gentil harlot and a kynde;/A bettre felawe sholde men noght fynde' (647–8). Though we may not consider him a 'good fellow', we are forced to recognise that opinions as to what does constitute such a person may vary.

Lastly, apart from Chaucer himself and the Host of the Tabard Inn who later decides to go on the pilgrimage, too, comes the **Pardoner**, the friend and companion of the Summoner. The Pardoner, who later (in the prologue to his tale) gives a very full account of how he goes about his professional activities, is a man who travels about selling pardons or 'indulgences' from the Pope which could – so he would claim – annul the sins of anyone who wanted to buy them. He also preaches. Chaucer seems to have hated pardoners, as Langland did, and he makes this one a repellent and contemptible figure. It soon becomes clear from the description which emphasises the Pardoner's effeminate physical characteristics, that he is a homosexual, and that his relationship with the Summoner is a perverted one. His hair and lack of a beard, his voice 'as smal as hath a goot' (688) as he sings his duet with the Summoner, and other similar details, hint at his true nature. Unattractive though he is with his thin yellow locks hanging over his shoulders, he is made even more unappealing by implicit comparison with the young Squire with

his curly hair and fresh colourful appearance, and by our realisation that
he wears no hood because he thinks his hair is worth displaying. Worse
still, though he is a very active, energetic pardoner, the 'holy' relics that
he carries with him are all bogus. From the pillow-case that he claims to
be the Virgin Mary's veil, down to the pig's bones that he presumably
passes off as relics of the saints, all the objects that he carries are used to
extort money from ignorant people. He deceives poor parish priests as
well as simple country congregations and takes for himself the money
that should go to help support the parson. But once again, as with the
other pilgrims, Chaucer indicates the Pardoner's superlative skill at his
work, giving not only an idea of his calling and what it involved, and
the criticisms often levelled against pardoners by earlier and
contemporary writers, but also a very vivid sketch of a unique individual
which enables us to take him to some extent at his own valuation.

When the pilgrims have all been introduced, Chaucer excuses himself
in advance for any displeasure that he may cause by attempting to report
accurately the uncensored words of his companions, and he also
apologises for not introducing the pilgrims in exactly the correct order.
We must realise, he explains, that he is not very clever – a comment
which must have amused his original audience, who presumably knew
him well. Then he introduces the Host, Harry Bailey, who unlike the
other members of the party, was a real person. The Host is both manly
and jolly, and a very competent organiser – other than this, we are not
told much about him. His character is to emerge in the course of the
pilgrimage, as he arranges the story-telling. At this point in the
proceedings, we see him put forward his plan: the teller of 'Tales of best
sentence and moost solaas' (798), or the most memorable and
entertaining stories, is to be rewarded with a free supper at the Tabard
on his return. When morning comes, we see the Host gathering the
pilgrims together, calling them by name, and arranging the casting of
lots for the first story-teller. By this means, Chaucer draws the reader
deeper into the imaginary world of the pilgrimage, and creates an
atmosphere of anticipation for what is to come.

The Knight's Tale

The Story

Duke Theseus, returning home with his bride and his sister Emily,
encounters a company of noble ladies grieving because they have been
deprived of the right to bury their husbands, killed in battle at Thebes.
To avenge them, he attacks Thebes and sacks it. Two princely young
knights, the cousins Palamon and Arcite, are rescued from a pile of
bodies and kept as prisoners by Theseus. One day they look out of their

tower, see Emily in the garden and both instantly fall in love with her. Later, Arcite is released and banished; but his longing for Emily is such that he soon returns disguised as a palace servant to be near her. Meanwhile Palamon eventually escapes, encounters Arcite in a wood and they fight furiously for Emily, just as Theseus rides by. The Duke is persuaded to pardon them, and arranges that they shall engage in a formal tournament for the hand of Emily in a year's time. In due course they return with their supporters and each goes to a temple to pray for help. In the ensuing contest, Palamon is defeated, but the gods intervene, and in the moment of victory, Arcite is thrown from his horse and mortally injured. His subsequent death, followed by an impressive funeral, causes deep grief. At last, however, the period of mourning ends and Theseus, after a speech advocating the acceptance of destiny and trust in loving providence, unites Palamon and Emily in the bond of marriage.

COMMENTARY: Chaucer took the story which later became *The Knight's Tale* from the *Teseida* of Boccaccio. He seems to have retold it some time before he began work on *The Canterbury Tales*, and then later refashioned it as an appropriate story for the Knight to tell. It is a tale of chivalry and romance, the rich and elaborate surface of which conceals a philosophical depth which makes it impressive and moving. In it, Chaucer confronts the problems that arise when two young men love the same girl, considers the role and function of the good ruler, and poses the question of how we are to make sense of a universe in which the innocent often have to suffer.

The Idea of Order

At the beginning of the tale, when Theseus is appealed to by the mourning ladies, he is moved to grant their request, and he attacks and sacks the city of Thebes, but we see that what gives the ladies satisfaction results in the misery of others. Palamon and Arcite are taken prisoner, and suffer in consequence; when later, both fall in love with Emily, it is clear that if one should have the joy of winning her, the other will be miserable. Palamon, in a soliloquy (1303–33), sees the cruelty of the gods as responsible for the fortuitous suffering of the innocent, and questions the order of the universe. Chaucer, through the operation of the pagan gods and goddesses and the figure of Theseus, ultimately suggests that there is meaning in the universe. Though the interplay of various forces represented principally by Fortune, Venus, Mars and Saturn, brings about both joy and sorrow in human affairs, these forces are ultimately under the control of a loving providence. All things in the universe are bound together by a chain of love – a dominant idea in *The Consolation of Philosophy* of Boethius which Chaucer had himself translated, and by which he was much influenced (see 'Chaucer's reading', page 34) – and human beings must accept the seeming arbitrariness of experience in the knowledge that order and meaning do exist in a scheme of things ultimately governed by providence, despite appearances to the contrary.

In *The Knight's Tale* Chaucer seems further to suggest that human beings must play their part in bringing order into apparent chaos. In Duke Theseus, he represents the good ruler who listens to the pleas of his subjects and endeavours to do justice. Moreover he tempers justice with mercy, and here women have a part to play, also. When Palamon and Arcite are discovered fighting in the forest, the pleading of his wife and sister persuade him to pardon the young men and arrange a tournament, in which it shall be decided in a more ordered way, who is to win Emily's hand. The theme of order and mercy is carried through when Theseus decrees that the tournament shall be fought, not to the death, but only to decide the winner; and when eventually Arcite dies, the wild grief of Palamon and Emily and the resigned acceptance of the aged Egeus contrasts with the calm efficiency with which Theseus organises the funeral, as he had organised the tournament. His long Boethian final speech on the chain of love emphasises the stability and order behind the mutability of this world; and in the perfect, lasting joy and accord with which he binds Palamon and Emily at last, he brings about the earthly counterpart of the divine harmony.

Love

Though Chaucer brings *The Knight's Tale* to a happy conclusion in the marriage of Palamon and Emily, it is an outcome not attained without suffering. At the moment of falling in love, Palamon goes pale and cries out, and Arcite is 'hurt as muche as he, or moore' (1116) when he sees Emily. Of course this is a stylised, symbolic, shorthand way of representing a more extended (and for many people still recognisable) experience of growing attraction and passionate, frustrated longing. It dramatically suggests Palamon's and Arcite's first realisation of the existence of the opposite sex and their own natural desire. Of course the experience brings pain because neither have what they both want so much. Each young man experiences an equally noble love for Emily, who knows nothing of either, and again (as earlier in *The Parliament of Fowls*) Chaucer confronts the problem of what is to be done when two equally acceptable lovers are in love with the same girl. As Theseus with a wry humour points out to Palamon and Arcite, 'Ye woot yourself she may nat wedden two/Atones . . . she may nat now han bothe' (1835–9); yet if each truly loves Emily, with genuine love, as distinct from feeling mere sexual attraction, the loser in the contest will be left deeply and permanently unhappy. Chaucer demands the sympathetic involvement of lovers in the audience by explicitly asking at the end of the first part of the poem, 'Who hath the worse, Arcite or Palamon?' (1378), when one can see Emily every day from his prison, while the other is free but banished. Yet the poem implicitly explores and questions other aspects of love as well, especially when it is read in conjunction with *The Miller's Tale* which follows it. In the latter story, two young men are attracted to the same young married woman, and the more dynamic of the two soon devises an ingenious way to satisfy his (and her) desires, despite the jealous care of her elderly husband. Such crude lustfulness contrasts with the enduring, idealised and idealising love of Arcite and Palamon, who 'serve' Emily for years with little hope of reward, but it also draws attention to an element of absurdity in the very intensity of the nobler emotion. The love that Palamon and Arcite experience, however, can be seen as counterpart of the love that binds the universe and maintains it in harmony.

The setting and background

Chaucer sets *The Knight's Tale* in ancient Athens; his Duke Theseus is the very same who married Hippolyta in Shakespeare's *A Midsummer Night's Dream*. Yet at the same time, as elsewhere in his writing, Chaucer brilliantly blends the classical world with a medieval setting which would have been familiar to his readers. At the beginning of the story, Theseus attacks Thebes, with a ruthlessness typical of medieval warfare, and the pillagers ransacking the heaps of dead bodies for spoil (as they must often have done in the Hundred Years' War with France) discover Palamon and Arcite still alive, and deliver them up to Theseus for ransom or imprisonment. The building of the lists for the tournament, described in great detail in the third part of the tale, suggests familiar medieval scenes. All the splendour and romance of chivalry accompany the mode of contest appointed by Theseus to decide who shall marry Emily, but when afterwards Arcite dies, Theseus erects a funeral pyre for him, the gods and demi-gods of the woodland flee in alarm from the grove where it is built, and the ceremony is followed by funeral games in the classical tradition. Chaucer, here as elsewhere, successfully fuses the classical and medieval worlds, harmonises the pagan and Christian elements in his story and communicates a serious message to his contemporaries.

The gods

One of the most striking features of *The Knight's Tale* is the description in Part 3 of the temples to which Palamon, Arcite and Theseus go to pray before the tournament takes place. These are dedicated to Venus, Mars and Diana, and each is described in elaborate detail. While they were of course classical deities appropriate to the general background of the tale, they were also known to Chaucer's contemporaries as names of the planets (as was Saturn later in the story) and of the moon. Since medieval people believed that the planets exercised powerful influences over life on this earth, affecting the destinies of individuals and nations, and even affecting inanimate objects such as plants and metals, Chaucer could fit these pagan deities into his story; for it was generally agreed that they acted, under God's control, to bring about the various situations and encounters and seemingly chance events of everyday life. In *The Knight's Tale*, through Theseus's final speech, we eventually see that the operation of these deities, or planets or forces, is neither hostile to man nor arbitrary, but under the control of the 'First Moevere' (2987), or Primum Mobile, the force of destiny by which the ultimate power in the universe, God, causes the heavenly bodies to move and exert their influence. We must believe, suggests Theseus, that the adverse events which occur in our lives, in the end work together for good, in a universe controlled ultimately by love. Thus, although the deities are classical in name and have their pagan temples, the scheme into which they are fitted is really a Christian one. The goddess Fortune, of whom the mourning ladies at the beginning of the tale complain, had become a favourite medieval image – assimilated into the Christian world view – for the means by which, under God, chance events come about in human lives.

When Palamon, Arcite and Emily pray to their deities, all their prayers are granted. Arcite, for example, later achieves the victory for which he prays to Mars; it is not, however, victory that he really wants, but Emily. Chaucer draws attention in the tale to the difficulty of knowing what to pray and strive for, and of knowing the real implications of our desires and prayers ('We witen nat what thing we prayen heere' (1260)), and in this way he indicates the complexity of human life and experience. This point is reinforced by the descriptions of the temples in which the prayers are offered. The details may at first glance seem to be merely decorative, but they add up to a very comprehensive impression of the experience associated with the dominant concept. Thus in the temple of Venus are depicted the inevitable sufferings associated with love, as well as its joys; in the temple of Mars, not only the glory and glamour of victory and chivalry, but the horrors of war and all that accompanies hatred and violence of any kind: 'The smylere with the knyf under the cloke . . . The tresoun of the mordrynge in the bedde' (1999–2001).

Symbols and images

In *The Knight's Tale*, symbolism helps to communicate Chaucer's meaning. Most strikingly, the images of tower and garden are more than merely the geographical locations for the captured Palamon and Arcite and for Emily. From the tower, in which they are confined, they look out on the garden in which Emily walks, unaware even of their existence; and we become aware that the tower is a symbol for the limited outlook of childhood, the garden for the wider possibilities of the adult world, leading out into a still wider world which includes the forest. The garden in medieval literature is frequently a symbolic location for significant encounters (as is the Garden of Eden, in the Bible, in which Adam and Eve were tempted by Satan), and Palamon's and Arcite's 'encounter' with Emily as she walks in it is perhaps more effective for being entirely a psychological experience. Later we see them in the forest, the unregulated, unrestricted area, fighting like wild beasts as their animal passions dominate them.

The characters in *The Knight's Tale* are sometimes felt to be disappointing because they are unrealistic, but it should be realised that they are the symbolic characters that the story itself requires. As it is partly a story about the unfairness and seeming arbitrariness of life, it needs two almost identical heroes: why *should* Arcite die, and never have the happiness of marriage with Emily? Why should the no more deserving Palamon be the fortunate one? Emily, though a beautiful and desirable girl, has as little character as it is possible for a heroine to have. But that is as it should be: the whole point is that neither Palamon nor Arcite know her at all, so that she represents for them their adult heart's desire, the most beautiful thing they have ever seen, the very embodiment of a young man's dream, which they are prepared to risk everything to realise.

The style

The Knight's Tale seems a very appropriate tale for the Knight to tell. It is serious and philosophical, concerned with chivalry and love in its most ideal form, and its setting is a courtly one. For such a story-teller and such a subject, Chaucer chose the high style, making the tale rich, dignified, and rather stylised. The action takes place over many years, allowing time for the characters to emerge into adulthood from adolescence (for example, Emily prays in the temple (2297–330) 'noght to ben a wyf and be with childe', though at the end of the poem she appears to be ready for her marriage to Palamon). Because of the long time-span of the story, it is necessarily slow-moving, particularly in contrast with the Miller's and Reeve's tales that follow it. The elaborate descriptions of the temples, of the lists, and of Arcite's funeral further enrich it and slow it down, but the function of these is more than merely ornamental. Where Chaucer seems most conventional and unrealistic (as for example in the portrait of Emily in the garden) it is usually because he is giving us a sense not of a particular but of a representative and typical experience.

The style of *The Knight's Tale* is very visual, reminding us of medieval pictures: the line of kneeling ladies when Theseus returns, the fierce fighting at Thebes, Emily in the garden, are just a few examples of this. Chaucer several times makes use of the rhetorical device of *occupatio* to enrich the poem: the Knight says that he will *not* tell us how 'wonnen was the regne of Femenye . . And how asseged was Ypolita . . . And of the feste that was at hir weddynge' (877–83), though in effect he gives us a good idea of previous events while saying that he has not got time to tell us. By this device, Chaucer also makes us aware that we are in the hands of a story-teller, not simply reading a story. 'I have, God woot, a large feeled to ere [to plough]' (886), says the Knight at the beginning of this tale. The technique maintains a rapport between teller and audience, giving it its own kind of immediacy and its own expectations – we know that this is the *Knight's* tale. However, though in many ways the tale is appropriate to its teller, it must be realised that in allotting it to the Knight, Chaucer is not attempting to reveal the Knight's personality in any depth through it.

The Miller's Prologue and Tale

When the Knight has finished his tale, the Host intends that the Monk should be the next story-teller, but the Miller (who was drunk by this time) insists on telling his tale to counterbalance the Knight's. It is, of course, the tale of a crude uneducated person, and Chaucer says that though he must relate it just as it was told, those who do not like it must turn the page and choose another tale.

The story

An old Oxford carpenter, named John, has a student, Nicholas, for a lodger, who is very good at predicting the weather. He also has a pretty young wife, Alison, for whom Nicholas has a great desire, as also does Absolon, the parish clerk. Alison is attracted to Nicholas, who devises a plan to enable them to make love. He shuts himself up in his room and pretends that he has had a divine warning that there will be a great flood. He advises John to get three large tubs and to hang them from the roof in his attic so that when the flood comes, he, Alison and Nicholas can float away to safety in them. John takes this advice, and on the night that the flood is supposed to come, all three get into their tubs. John is soon asleep, and then Nicholas and Alison climb down and go to bed together. Meanwhile Absolon comes round to serenade Alison beneath the low window of her bedroom. He asks her for a kiss, but when she comes to the window, it is not her face but her behind that she puts out for him to kiss in the darkness. Realising his mistake, he rushes away disgusted, seeking revenge. He gets a red-hot plough-share from the blacksmith and returns to the window, asking for another kiss. This time Nicholas comes to repeat the joke and Absolon repays him by applying the hot iron to his bare bottom. In agony Nicholas yells 'water, water'. John thinks the flood has come and cuts the ropes that held up his tub, crashing down and breaking his arm. When the neighbours rush out, Alison and Nicholas tell them that John thought there was a flood, so they all laugh at him and think he is mad.

COMMENTARY: The situation in *The Miller's Tale* parallels that in *The Knight's Tale*, in so far as in it there are two young men who are rivals for the same girl. But whereas *The Knight's Tale*, shows a pure and noble love expressing itself in patient service and devotion, *The Miller's Tale* shows the lengths to which people may be prepared to go merely to get into bed together. It is the tale of a coarse, sensual churl who knows nothing about love, and cannot distinguish between it and lust. The tales complement each other, however, in showing two quite different kinds of love-situation. The love of Palamon and Arcite for Emily is admirable, but it has its touches of absurdity: for Emily, the object of their passionate devotion, knows nothing of either of them. The lust of Nicholas and Absolon for Alison, on the other hand, has nothing in common with the worship that the lovers of *The Knight's Tale* offer to Emily, though of course Palamon and Arcite also ultimately desire sexual satisfaction. Taking the tales together, then, we see the rich diversity of human nature through very different sexual relationships. *The Miller's Tale* is a parody of *The Knight's Tale*, and while the latter is a courtly romance, *The Miller's Tale* belongs to the genre of *fabliau*. This was a type of story, very popular in France, in which jealous husbands were frequently outwitted by clever young priests or students. Chaucer probably heard or read some version of the story and decided to make use of it himself, retelling it with such superb timing and brilliant use of visual images as to make it one of his greatest technical achievements.

Narrative technique

To make this unlikely tale carry the utmost conviction, and achieve the greatest possible effect, Chaucer pays very careful attention to detail. He sets the scene in Oxford, where clever, lively young men would naturally be found. He indicates Nicholas's reputation for forecasting the weather so that John will believe him when he predicts the flood. He shows us exactly how everything was situated: the cat-hole in Nicholas's door through which the boy can see him gazing upwards, as if in a visionary trance, the tubs hanging in the attic, the low window to which Absolon comes, and so forth.

The characters

Chaucer also depicts the characters in this tale very vividly and he carefully individualises them. Whereas Emily in *The Knight's Tale* is the ideal heroine of romance, symbolic rather than real, Alison is a very lively country girl. Chaucer describes her dress in great detail, giving an impression of a provincial lack of taste, but above all, he emphasises qualities that associate her with attractive young animals. It is natural for her to want to mate with another attractive young animal, rather than with her elderly husband. She is fresh and fragrant, associated with country things, and her description builds up a strong impression of a rural as opposed to a courtly setting.

Absolon is also vividly realised. He is effeminate but versatile: he can sing, dance, and act after a fashion and he pays great attention to his appearance, wearing bright-coloured clothes and combing his long golden hair carefully. He appears to rate his own charms and accomplishments more highly than other people do, for when he is serenading Alison in what he seems to think is an elegant way, she thinks he is just a fool. Chaucer stresses one other significant aspect of his personality: he is very fastidious, with a particular dislike of unpleasant smells, and he is obsessed with anything to do with the mouth, which makes the unpleasant fate that befalls him all the more disagreeable for him.

Nicholas, on the other hand, is not presented in physical detail, appropriately, for it is his cleverness – though unfortunately for him, he is not quite clever enough – that is his predominating characteristic. Chaucer refers to him again and again as 'hende Nicholas', and this word 'hende' that had once meant 'noble' in courtly literature is used to good effect here. The word had gone down in the world, so to speak, and had become old-fashioned and provincial, meaning little more than 'nice', and it indicates the quality that Alison admires. It also has connotations of 'handy', 'near at hand' and Nicholas is not only quick to put his hands on Alison (3276), but is also 'near at hand' at all appropriate times. He has other accomplishments, too, of course: like Absolon, he is musical, and is to be heard singing a lyric about the visit of the archangel Gabriel to the Virgin Mary, of which a version has survived to the present day. With such realistic touches, Chaucer adds to the mass of convincing detail which gives substance to this story.

John, the elderly carpenter, is presented as a stupid and credulous husband and Chaucer, whose sympathy for women is always apparent, does not allow us to feel very favourably towards him, since he was asking for trouble in marrying a young wife. John is foolish enough to believe that there will be another great flood, like the one in the Bible, which only Noah and his family survived. He should have known better, for God had promised, in that story, that there would never be another such flood and it was arrogant of him to suppose (even if there were to be another flood) that he was singled out to be warned and saved. One of the most amusing passages in the tale occurs when Nicholas is telling John of the flood to come, and John goes about providing the tubs, as a means of avoiding destruction.

The style

The Miller's Tale is as complete a contrast to *The Knight's Tale* as it could be, not only in its story, its value and the type of 'love' that it demonstrates, but also in the way in which it is told. It is fast moving where *The Knight's Tale* is slow, and its action covers only a few days instead of a great many years. Even so, Chaucer varies the pace of the narration within the tale, slowing it down when Nicholas has his 'vision' and explains to John about the imaginary flood to come, leading up to the final catastrophic sequence of events which follow in very quick succession. There is a wealth of concrete visual detail, as in *The Knight's Tale*, but it is realistic rather than symbolic, enabling us to imagine just how everything would have happened.

The effect is also enhanced by naturalistic dialogue. When Nicholas, at the beginning of the tale, catches hold of Alison, she exclaims 'lat be, Nicholas,/Or I wol crie "out, harrow" and "allas"!' (3285–6) – a merely token protest. When Absolon comes serenading, she repulses him with a crude contempt that should have warned him to go away: '"Go fro the wyndow, Jakke fool", she sayde' (3708); and later when he has been punished more materially she is still more vulgarly forthright '"Tehee!" quod she, and clapte the wyndow to' (3740). Absolon hurries off, plotting revenge, and has a brisk exchange of dialogue with the smith (3765–84), which contrasts with the fanciful terms of his earlier love-song to Alison when he had called her his 'hony-comb', sweet Alisoun,/My faire bryd, my sweete cynamome' (3698–9).

Parody

The Miller's Tale is made the more effective by the elements of parody which add another dimension, and make it much more than just a very well told, rather crude story. It parodies the values, the situations and even some of the techniques and language of courtly romance. Nicholas offers his 'lady' a very different kind of service from that offered by Palamon and Arcite, and the offerings that Absolon sees as appropriate to make to Alison to win her love consist of 'pyment, meeth, and spiced ale,/ And wafres, pipyng hoot' (3378–9), all forms of food and drink, as well as 'meede' (money). What the 'nye, slye' Nicholas values in Alison is not the well-bred reserve of the courtly lady, but the lively enthusiasm with which she accedes to his wish to seduce her. The element of parody is also apparent in the other ways in which the two young men go about the task of making an impression on Alison by their manly prowess, Nicholas by his elaborate planning and Absolon by his impersonation of Herod in the local production of the miracle plays, as well as by his serenading.

In Absolon Chaucer further gives us a delightfully absurd parody of the courtly lover. His false refinement, affectation and effeminacy take the place of noble bearing and courage, and his ridiculous 'love-longynge' (3679) which makes him 'moorne as dooth a lamb after the tete' (3704) and unable to 'ete na moore than a mayde' (3707) parodies the nobler sentiments of more aristocratic lovers.

Alison, too, presents a most ingenious parody of the courtly heroine. Traditionally, poets had described the peerless beauty of such ladies, whose perfect proportions and lovely complexions, matchless eyes and golden hair made them irresistible. Chaucer concentrates on the features of Alison's appearance that no lady would have, such as her apron. Her smock, her shoes laced high up so as to show her legs, are things that a courtly heroine would not wish to have revealed. We are not told about Alison's hair (as her eye-brows are black, presumably it is unromantically dark), but instead we hear how her forehead shone when she had washed after work. All the comparisons, moreover, remind us of the countryside and farmyard and so de-glamorise Alison: she is slender as a weasel, her apron white as milk, she is softer than wool from a sheep, and her song is like that of a swallow sitting on a barn (Emily in *The Knight's Tale* sings in a heavenly way, like an angel). Finally, Alison is not like a lily or a rose, but resembles a flower called unromantically, a pig's-eye; and she would be highly suitable either for a lord to go to bed with, or equally for a mere yeoman to marry.

The Reeve's Prologue and Tale

Between the end of *The Miller's Tale* and the beginning of the next comes a linking passage which describes the reaction (mostly favourable) of the pilgrims to *The Miller's Tale*, and allows the angry Reeve to utter some grumbling and gloomy remarks. The Host tells him to leave off preaching and tell his tale, which the Reeve carefully selects in order to get his own back on the Miller. This link between the tales gives a sense of the ongoing pilgrimage and of real-life reactions on the part of those present to the tales told.

The story

At Trumpington near Cambridge there is a miller proud of the fact that his wife is the daughter of a local parson, and of what in consequence, he considers the high birth of their twenty-year-old daughter. One day two poor young scholars from the North, John and Alan, come to get corn ground for their college. They watch the miller carefully, for he has a reputation for stealing corn, but when the corn is safely ground, they find that their horse has run away. When at last they catch it, they find the miller has stolen some of their corn, and as it is night, they cannot return to Cambridge. The miller offers them supper and a bed for the night and eventually, after drinking much ale, they all go to bed in the miller's one and only bedroom. Alan, kept awake by the miller's snoring, decides to get into bed with the miller's daughter; and John not wanting to seem lacking in enterprise, moves the baby's cradle from the end of the bed in which the miller and his wife sleep, to the end of his own. When later the miller's wife has to get up, she comes back to John's bed by mistake, groping for the cradle, and John takes full advantage of his opportunity. Some time later Alan, returning to his bed, gets in with the miller, thinking he is John, and tells him what he has been doing. A terrible fight ensues, but eventually the miller has the worst of it. Alan and John return to Cambridge with their corn, having successfully triumphed over him in the end.

COMMENTARY: Like *The Miller's Tale*, *The Reeve's Tale* is a *fabliau*, in which we see clever young men outwitting a cunning, self-satisfied husband. Though Chaucer tells the tale with very great skill, it does not have the richness of *The Miller's Tale*, largely because it lacks the element of parody. Its plot, however, is very neatly and elegantly worked out, its characters have just the right amount of individuality, and it slowly gathers momentum, until after the tremendous fight in the bedroom it subsides into calm satisfaction on the part of the victorious students, and of its teller, the Reeve.

Narrative technique

Chaucer's careful attention to the setting helps to motivate the action of this tale. The mill is located just far enough outside Cambridge for it to be dangerous for Alan and John to try to go back through the fens after dark. The fact that they are Cambridge students who pride themselves on their watchful intelligence enhances the humour: first they find themselves less clever than they thought when their horse is let loose and their corn stolen. Then they find – in the end – that what they have to pride themselves on are their physical rather than their mental powers. Chaucer indicates so precisely the lay-out of the miller's bedroom, with its three big beds and the baby's cradle, that it is easy to visualise exactly how the amazing and complicated events of that unrestful night occur.

Characters

The story generates the characters it needs. The cunning, jealous miller who thinks himself a match for the two young men is full of ridiculous pride because his wife is the illegitimate daughter of a parson, and his pretensions are further enhanced by the parson's intention of marrying his granddaughter well and making her his heir, to honour his 'hooly blood' (3985).

Alan and John, who regard themselves as a couple of quick-witted lads, are unlike the sophisticated 'hende Nicholas' in *The Miller's Tale*, with his books and musical and scientific instruments, and they use northern forms of speech when they talk; '"Symond," quod John, "by God, nede has na peer./Hym boes serve hymself that has na swayn"' (4026–7). Here the form 'boes' (behoves) and 'na' (no) show that they speak a rather different dialect from the standard southern one of the miller. Alan and John are not differentiated from each other, or individualised in the way that Nicholas and Absolon are in the previous tale, however.

This rather heartless tale of the puncturing of unjustified pretentions is made more amusing by its ironies. The miller, for example, when he is offering the students supper and a bed for the night, says that their learning and powers of argument will enable them to 'make a place/A myle brood of twenty foot of space' (4123–4). The events of the night consequently show that the 'art' they have learned is of a different order and all that they do rather diminishes the room than expands it.

The Cook's Prologue and Tale

The Cook, who says that his name is Hogge (or Roger) of Ware, is maliciously delighted by *The Reeve's Tale* because it shows a miller set in his place, and he offers to contribute next. The Host, in accepting the offer, comments on the bad food that the Cook sells, though he begs him not to take offence at his remarks, for 'A man may seye ful sooth in game and pley' (4355). The observation can be related more generally to such tales as the Miller's and Reeve's; in them Chaucer does 'seye ful sooth', in showing, albeit through the form of fantasy, something not only of the great diversity of human behaviour, but more subtly the workings of the human mind that likes to liberate itself from the pressures of everyday reality with such fantasies.

The Cook's Tale unfortunately did not get completed, though it seems to have been intended to be similar in genre to the Miller's and Reeve's. It begins with a lively but dishonest London apprentice called Perkyn, who is dismissed by his master and goes to live with a friend. There the story ends.

The Man of Law's Introduction, Prologue and Tale

As the pilgrims continue on their way, the Host becomes very much aware of time passing (it is 10.00 a.m. on 18 April) and urges his hearers never to waste time. He calls on the Man of Law to tell a story, but he says that he will find it difficult, because Chaucer has already told all the good tales in some book or other, and he gives a list of the stories in Chaucer's *The Legend of Good Women*. Then, saying that he will tell his tale in prose, after a short sententious prologue, he begins.

The story

(1) Some Syrian merchants on returning home from Rome, tell their Sultan of the beauty and goodness of the Emperor's daughter Constance. His desire to make her his wife is so great that he is baptised so as to remove religious obstacles, and a match is arranged. Constance, with great sorrow, has to leave her parents and sail to Syria.

(2) Here she is married to the Sultan, but his mother, angered by her son's conversion, has him and his followers killed and Constance put into a rudderless ship. God hears her prayers and protects her, and after three years, she safely reaches the coast of Northumberland. Here, she is looked after by the constable and eventually the King, Alla, falls in love with her and marries her. However, Alla's mother hates her and when Constance has a child while Alla is away, she tampers with the messages, so that Constance is put into her ship again with her baby son, upon the open sea.

(3) Alla, when he discovers what has happened, kills his wicked mother, while Constance, protected by God, sails on. After various adventures, she reaches Rome, where she lives with her rescuer, a senator, and her little son. When Alla comes on pilgrimage to Rome, he chances to see his child and is joyfully reunited with Constance, and she with her father the Emperor. They then return to England, but a year later Alla dies, and Constance goes back to Rome, where with her father she lives a happy and holy life ever after.

COMMENTARY: Chaucer read this pious tale in an Anglo-French version by Nicholas Trivet written about 1335, and though it has less appeal for the modern reader than many of the other *Canterbury Tales*, he must have valued it himself, or he would not have produced a new version for inclusion in his collection. Such a tale did not give him scope for the exercise of his greatest powers, but it would have been appreciated by his original hearers, who would have believed – as would also have Chaucer – that it was a true story of how God looks after those who put their trust in him. It is a good example of the kind of story that medieval people much enjoyed – a moral tale, from which they felt that they could learn much that was helpful to them in their inner, spiritual lives. At the same time, the adventures of Constance, like all such adventures in folk-tale and romance, have a satisfying quality. Virtue ultimately triumphs, the evil characters are destroyed, and in various ways – natural and supernatural – Constance is delivered from all her troubles. The simple, repetitive plot is patterned to arouse and to allay suspense, and to bring the story of Constance back full circle to its starting point at the Emperor's court in Rome, all perils and sorrows past. The typical motifs of folk-tale are effective: the Sultan's obsessive desire for the unseen bride, the wicked mother-figure, the treacherous messenger, the casting of mother and child into the ship, the recognition scene after long separation. These motifs with which we are familiar from traditional stories have, of course, a truth to life of their own, on their own particular level: mothers-in-law are not usually as loving as mothers, for example; messengers may in real life be motivated to tamper with messages. Such motifs may be recognised and accepted as meaningful in a general way; they would, of couse, be compatible with the particularities of character and of time and place of such stories as the Miller's and Reeve's if made to play a large part, but they fit quite happily into *The Man of Law's Tale*, where character and situation are not given the same kind of sharply-etched reality.

Though it is without philosophical depth, the story is distinguished by delicate, affecting touches of pathos which Chaucer's human sympathy, particularly for the suffering of women, often provides in his poems. Constance's sadness when she has to leave her parents, whom she expects never to see again, for marriage to the Sultan is poignantly communicated. When she is accused of murder by an enemy and brought before the King, Chaucer describes her appearance by comparing her to a victim being led to his death:

Have ye nat seyn somtyme a pale face,
Among a prees, of hym that hath be lad
Toward his deeth . . .
Men myghte knowe his face that was bistad,
Amonges alle the faces in that route? (645–50)

Such a passage stands out in a tale in which a more comprehensively realistic technique would be out of place.

The Wife of Bath's Prologue and Tale

Because no single manuscript survives in which we have Chaucer's finished arrangement of such of *The Canterbury Tales* as he was able to complete before his death, it is difficult to know in what order he intended them to be read. After *The Man of Law's Tale*, it is generally thought by editors, as in Robinson's edition, that the Wife of Bath's should follow.

The Wife of Bath's Prologue

The Wife of Bath embarks upon a long account and justification of her marriages to five successive husbands, three of them old and two young men, all of whom (with the possible exception of the fifth) have in turn died. She is interrupted early on by the Pardoner, who says he has been thinking of marrying but now doubts whether he should. When the story of her married life is concluded, the Friar and the Summoner begin to show their dislike of each other, and the Host interposes to urge the Wife to tell her actual tale.

COMMENTARY: Chaucer drew on the vast amount of misogynistic clerical writing available in the Middle Ages for the Wife of Bath's Prologue. From the dismal denunciations of women and the extensive catalogues of their vices and weaknesses composed by these authorities on the subject, he makes a superbly comic and vital exposition of the Wife of Bath's view of the short-comings and faults of husbands; and in doing so, he proves how right the misogynistic writers were in their accusations against women, if the Wife of Bath is anything to go by.

The Wife of Bath asserts her individuality with great zest, by emphasising the validity of experience – personal experience – in an age when 'auctoritee', the acknowledged authority of learned writers in the past, was considered to be the best guide and of the greatest significance. She knows all about the 'wo that is in marriage' (3) she says. She questions and challenges the teaching of the Bible, quoting examples from the Old and New Testaments, to justify the fact that she has been five times married and would be ready to welcome a sixth husband. In the fourteenth century, when a high proportion of men, monks, friars, priests and others, were committed to a celibate life, books which decried women, the daughters of Eve, as temptresses and instruments of the devil were naturally popular, and the virtue of virginity was much exalted. The Wife goes on to justify her antipathy for virginity by arguing among other things that not everyone can be perfect, that household utensils cannot all be made of gold, and that God would not have given human beings sexual organs, if they were not meant to use them. The Pardoner's interruption of this general discourse invites her to 'teche us yonge men of youre praktike' (187) and gives her the opportunity of revealing, in detail, not so much how her husbands treated her, but how she treated them. So we see her not as the unfortunate victim of male dominance, but as an energetic and powerful exponent of women's liberation. As her tale unfolds, it becomes very clear that all the various charges levelled against women have been entirely justified in her case, and yet we cannot help sympathising with her, and half admiring the vibrant personality that Chaucer reveals through her own words.

The first three husbands
The Wife starts off with her three good, elderly, rich husbands, indicating how hard she made them work to give her pleasure in bed, and explains how she took them to task (235–382). First, she used to complain that she was less well-dressed than her neighbour, and would accuse her husband of paying too much attention to her neighbour and the maid. Then she would start on a long series of accusations that she claimed her husband had made against her (248–378). In this passage, the Wife says exactly what she said her husbands said against women in general, and against her in particular, telling them that they had been drunk when they made their complaints (381), and so did not remember what they had said.

The insistent, nagging voice of the Wife, determined to get in first and level her accusations before her partner could attack her, becomes a torrent of complaint against her dumbfounded husbands, and then subsides into the admission that 'al was fals' (382). Our response is ambiguous: we react sympathetically to the dynamic energy of the Wife's self-assertion, while we recognise how much her husbands must have suffered from the chiding wife who makes a man to flee out of his own house (279–80) (one of the disagreeable comments that she says her old husbands used to make to her). The Wife's Prologue, at a more general level, reminds us of the perversity of human nature in general, the inevitable dissatisfaction with our lot, as she reveals all the drawbacks of marriage, yet makes it clear that it is a more desirable way of life than celibacy.

Chaucer drew upon some learned works well-known in his time for these passages: the *Miroir de Mariage* of Eustache Deschamps, a French poet who addressed a complimentary poem to Chaucer; the *Epistola Adversus Jovinianum* by St Jerome (*c*. 340–420), a great early Christian scholar and writer; and the *Liber Aureolus de Nuptiis* of Theophrastus (which St Jerome quotes). Chaucer also uses the *Epistola Valerii ad Rufinum de non Ducenda Uxore* by Walter Map, a Welsh poet writing in

Latin about 1200. From these treatises, as from a pile of rubble, Chaucer's genius enables the Wife of Bath to emerge, very much alive and kicking, to put a woman's point of view in a male dominated age, and to win our sympathy. How does he work the transformation? It is easier to see what has happened than how the magic is performed. First of all the rhetorical pattern of repetition has a cumulative effect, as the Wife's false accusations mount up: 'Thou seist . . . Thanne seistow . . . Thus seistow . . .' and so on. The husband is given no chance to reply. We hear the very tone of voice and gain a strong sense of the speaker in the colloquial language and repeated questions: 'Why is my neighebores wyf so gay?' (236), 'What eyleth swich an old man for to chide?' (281) and in the exclamations: 'Sire old lecchour, lat thy japes be!' (242), 'a! benedicitee!' (280) etc. At the same time, in this part of her Prologue and elsewhere, the Wife's assertions build up a powerful impression of the world in which she lives – the ordinary, everyday, unromantic, uncourtly world of neighbours and servants, animals and household utensils, clothes, chests and beds and fireplaces and candles. The solid weight of concrete imagery, whether drawn from Chaucer's learned sources, or from homely proverbs, or from Chaucer's own invention, substantiates the Wife of Bath's milieu and way of life.

The Wife's account of her matrimonial technique is also made more effective by Chaucer's use of contrast. Sometimes the Wife even takes exception to the teachings of the Bible on the subject; sometimes – when it suits her purpose – she makes use, by contrast, of the teaching of 'authority': 'Deceite, wepynge, spynnyng God hath yive to wommen kyndley [by their nature]' (401–2). So she justifies her deception of her husbands. She casts her husbands' words in their teeth, urging them to practise the patience they preach (434–7) in a contrasting passage of feigned tenderness and generosity (431–449) when poor Wilkyn submits to her, recommending that, as men claim to be more reasonable than women and one of them must give way, it is he who should do so (440–2). Beyond the comic predicament of the poor husband, however, we glimpse the inescapable problems of such human relationships, of balancing the conflict of wills and clashes of personality almost inevitable in marriage.

The fourth and fifth husbands
The three elderly husbands disposed of, the Wife turns to the next, a very different kind of spouse, for he was a 'revelour' (453) and had a mistress, which she resented. This episode in her life enables her to look back to her youth with regret but also with satisfaction for, as she says,

It tikleth me aboute myn herte roote.
Unto this day it dooth myn herte boote
That I have had my world as in my tyme. (471–3).

The regret that her youth and beauty are gone is tempered by her positive determination to be 'myrie' (479) nevertheless, and to make the most of what she has left. Again we catch a glimpse of the commonplace world to which, fundamentally, she belongs, as she explains how she dealt with the misdemeanours of her fourth husband: 'In his owene grece I made hym frye' (487). She also made 'his shoo ful bitterly hym wrong' (492) – made his shoe pinch him, metaphorically speaking. And then her world opens up with her pilgrimage to Jerusalem, which – whatever it did for her – does not seem to have led to an increase in Christian charity.

The Wife's sense of the fundamental opposition between men and women, to a large extent eroded now, leads on to further analysis of the psychological differences between the sexes, and to the question of what women really want, asked and answered explicitly in the tale that follows. The fifth husband is the one that the Wife most loved; and that mainly because her husband's love was difficult to win. Again we see the social background to which she belongs, its coarseness (534), its amusements – listening to gossip, walking in the fields, going to church, to plays, to weddings, and dressing up for the occasion (545–62). With striking realism Chaucer allows her to get so absorbed in her recollections of a happy time in her life that she forgets what she was saying and where she had got to in the autobiography until she catches up with herself: 'A ha! by God, I have my tale ageyn' (586). The fifth husband, Jankyn, is a 'joly clerk' from Oxford, and half the age of his wife, possessed of such a fine pair of legs and feet that the infatuated Wife makes over all her possessions to him. His ownership of a highly prized book all about 'wikked wyves' (685) from which he has the amiable habit of reading aloud, leads to a tremendous scene. She tears three leaves from the precious book, and knocks him into the fire. He fells her to the ground with a blow which knocks her unconscious and almost kills her, and which leaves her deaf in one ear. In the end, however, they 'fille acorded' (812). This relationship, based firstly on physical compatibility and desire, seems to emerge from violent antagonism and conflict, as a result of the husband's readiness to submit to his wife's conditions and allow her 'al the soveraynetee' (818). She is to do as she likes, and look after the estate. She has got what she wants and can love in return, but perhaps her victory is not total: her deafness remains as a reminder of his ultimate physical superiority.

The learned works upon which Chaucer drew for some of his material have already been mentioned, but for the actual figure of the Wife, he was also to some extent indebted to the *Roman de la Rose* in which there is an old woman, La Vieille, whose expertise in matters of love foreshadows that of the Wife of Bath. The references to the *Roman* are not direct, as they are, for example, to the books by Walter Map and

Theophrastus (which he refers to as 'Valerie and Theofraste' (671)). The modern reader, impatient of references to so many unfamiliar classical and biblical characters and incidents, may react with impatience to lines 669–787, and regard them as a lapse on Chaucer's part. For his contemporaries, however, to whom books were not readily available, the passage would have held much more interest, as they recognised or were made aware of famous stories from the past. The passage is not without dramatic importance, too, for it enables Chaucer to establish a sense of mounting outrage and provocation until finally the Wife can endure no more, and maddened with indignation attacks book and husband together.

Astrology

In addition to such literary references, *The Wife of Bath's Prologue* also contains a number of astrological references. 'Venus me yaf my lust, my likerousness,/And Mars yaf me my sturdy hardynesse' (611–2), says the Wife, accounting for her dominant traits according to the best scientific knowledge of the day. Astrology also explains the antagonism between clerks and women, she comments, for clerks are the 'children of Mercurie' (697), while women are under the domination of Venus, 'Therefore no Womman of no clerk is preysed' (706).

Is it likely that a woman would have been so well-informed and well read as the Wife of Bath appears to be? Of course she is an exceptional person, and the 'sturdy hardynesse' that she derives from the influence of Mars gives her a masculine aggressiveness and force that enables her in some respects to enter the masculine world of learning, and draw on it for her arguments as she draws liberally on the more homely proverbial sayings with which she so often supports them. She is, however, a fictional character, not a faithful representation of fourteenth-century feminine achievement.

The Wife of Bath's Tale: the story

In the days of King Arthur a certain knight, riding through the countryside, encounters a maiden and rapes her. According to the law, he should be beheaded, but the queen and other ladies beg the king to spare his life, if he can, within a year, answer the question of what it is that women most desire. While listing some of the answers given to his enquiries, the Wife of Bath breaks off to tell the story of Midas and then continues. At the end of the year the knight, still without a satisfactory answer, sees some ladies dancing in a forest, who then vanish leaving only an old crone. She asks him what he is seeking, offering to help him, and as a result he is able to give the right answer to the queen. When he does so, the crone comes forward and asks for his hand in marriage as her reward. Unable to refuse, he is married to her, but with shame and loathing. When they are in bed, he writhes away from her in disgust; and she reproaches him for his arrogance, pointing out that the noble qualities that he said she lacks come from God alone, not from high birth. She similarly disposes of his objection to her poverty and age, and gives him a choice: to have his wife hideous, old and true to him, or young, beautiful and false. He wisely leaves the choice to her, and she instantly becomes beautiful, young and true, so that they lived happily ever after.

COMMENTARY: The story on which Chaucer based *The Wife of Bath's Tale* was a well-known popular one. It is an *exemplum* or story to illustrate the particular point that what women most want is their own way. Chaucer's friend and contemporary, the poet John Gower (?1330–1408), wrote a version of the tale, differing from Chaucer's in that his knight did not commit rape at the beginning, and the dilemma with which he is finally confronted is the less complex one of whether to have his wife fair by day and foul by night, or the reverse. Chaucer's version allows deeper and subtler meanings to emerge, as a result of his insight into human nature and skilful handling of the material.

The opening of the tale, in King Arthur's days, provides the 'once upon a time' setting that can accommodate magic, as well as allowing the Wife of Bath's voice to be heard in a sarcastic jibe at the activities of friars which prepares for the knight's misdemeanour. The rape is taken with appropriate seriousness nevertheless, for 'swich clamour' (889) arises in consequence, that he is threatened with the penalty of death. At this point we see the operation of mercy rather than justice, as the queen and the other ladies intercede to allow the knight a reprieve. In true fairy-tale manner, the task set him seems irrelevant, but it allows the story to take up the theme of *The Wife of Bath's Prologue*, and relates to his crime, in that he had forced upon a woman what she did *not* want. As the knight pursues his task, we are kept aware of the Wife's involvement with her story, as she interpolates her own point of view: 'A man shal wynne us best with flaterye' (932). She is reminded of the story of Midas and his ass's ears, and asks the pilgrims if they wish to hear his tale, a device which keeps us aware that we are being told a story, and which also allows time to elapse. And then the year is up; the knight sadly turns homeward and comes upon the dancing ladies and the foul old hag. The suspense mounts as the moment of disclosure approaches, the knight is saved and the old hag claims her reward. Now he has to suffer, as he had made a woman suffer the year before, and he voices what she must have wished, 'Taak al my good, and lat my body go' (1061). He is shamed and wretched, forced to go to bed with the loathsome bride to whom he is joined for life, and so embarrassed that all day long he 'hidde hym as an owle' (1081). His wife smilingly taunts him, reminding him that she has saved his life, but her repulsiveness, old age and humble rank are more than he can bear to be associated with.

At this point Chaucer brings a new dimension into the popular tale, as the hag addresses the knight on the subject of 'gentilesse'. She tells him that only those who perform 'gentil dedes' (1115) are entitled to be regarded as noble, for nobility is not a matter of high birth or riches. 'Gentilesse' comes from Christ himself (1117), from God alone, and shows itself in consideration for others – again she emphasises that 'he is gentil that dooth gentil dedis' (1170), and she asserts her equality with the knight and her claim to be considered of equal rank. The knight is not entitled to privilege and respect, unless he can make his conduct as noble as the rank he claims. The accusation of poverty is similarly rebutted: Christ himself lived a life of poverty, and so that state is not to be despised, particularly as it is not a pleasant state to be in. Poverty has been praised by philosophers as enabling a man to know his God, himself and his true friends. And finally, says the old hag, age is not to be despised either, but respected for its wisdom.

This dialogue gives the story a moral and social dimension, in its reminder that true nobility cannot be inherited, but is a matter of individual responsibility and personal effort, and that it must have spiritual origins. True nobility means loving your neighbour as yourself, regardless of rank. When the knight, suitably chastened, is given his choice, Chaucer again introduces a new element. In its original form, the story offered him a simpler choice, relating to what Chaucer has already stressed, his embarrassment and shame at becoming the husband of a foul hag. The simpler choice was based on a joke about sexual pride: would you prefer to be envied and admired because you possess a lovely bride when in reality you do not, or despised because your bride is hideous when in secret she is beautiful? Chaucer, in making the choice include faithfulness or the reverse, makes it a more profound one, more closely related to real life and to real personal relationships. In the choice presented by the simpler version, it was possible to possess a beautiful wife, though perhaps only in secret; in Chaucer's it would not be possible to *possess* a beautiful wife, even in secret, for she would in any case be untrue. The choice before Chaucer's knight involves the balancing of faithfulness and love, albeit from a repulsive creature, against the doubtful advantage of seeming to possess a prize which in fact you do not, and which other people know that you do not. There is no way in which the knight can now really possess a beautiful bride, either by day or by night. If he chooses a bride who is beautiful and faithless, his shame – the fact that he is a cuckold – will inevitably be known. He has enjoyed a beautiful young girl in the past, against her will, and now can have no more such pleasure unless he literally and symbolically allows a woman to make the choice.

No wonder the knight finds it impossible to decide and allows his wife to make the choice for him! By allowing her the sovereignty that all women want, he shows that he has actually learnt the meaning of the answer he had given the queen, instead of merely repeating it parrot-fashion. He gets the beautiful bride, the credit for having married her, and the faithful wife as well. Does he deserve them? Maybe not, but he has suffered and perhaps expiated the crime he had committed and is a reformed character. He no longer tries to impose his will on a woman, he allows the woman to choose for herself in the matter of personal relationships. Through the fairy-tale, with its magical elements, Chaucer is able to illustrate 'gentilesse' in action: sympathetic awareness of and respect for other people's needs and wishes, for, as he says in *The Knight's Tale*, 'gentil mercy oghte passen right' (3089).

The story ends with the magical transformation and the bliss that ensues. The knight has submitted, but now his wife obeys him in everything (1255) – a situation hardly in accord with the Wife of Bath's precepts. Now, her tale done, she re-asserts herself as the sex-obsessed, domineering woman of her Prologue:

> . . . Jhesu Crist us sende
> Housbondes meeke, yonge, and fresshe abedde,
> And grace t'overbyde hem that we wedde (1258–60)

She misses the point of her own story, so to speak, because it is not part of Chaucer's intention to make the tale expressive of the teller's personality and attitudes. It is only loosely appropriate to the Wife of Bath. At the simplest level, the point of the story – that what women want is their own way – is well suited to the Wife of Bath's outlook, while it makes the stock anti-feminist joke; but the ending of the tale carries the implications further, into the realm of more complex real-life personal relationships, which must depend upon mutuality.

The characters

As in all good fairy-tales, the characters in *The Wife of Bath's Tale* have no individuality and do not even have names, because they do not need them. It is what the knight does, rather than who he is, that matters; it is a story about human behaviour, not an individual character study. Nor is the old hag who becomes a lovely young bride to be seen as in some way representing the Wife of Bath: her sentiments on 'gentilesse' hardly agree with the general attitudes of the Wife. We are, however, very much aware of the Wife as story-teller expounding her story, up to the point at which the knight approaches the end of his search (983). The story then takes over and virtually excludes its teller until the Wife bounces back with her prayer for meek husbands. It is not of course, a realistic story, but its power to communicate deeper meaning is almost equal to that of myth, a form with which it is associated.

The Friar's Prologue and Tale

In the linking passage which follows *The Wife of Bath's Tale*, the Friar is seen to be continually glaring at the Summoner, though at first he refrains from expressing his animosity. However, he offers to tell a tale about a summoner, and begins to be very insulting. The Host begs him to get on with it and leave the Summoner alone, while the Summoner says that the Friar can say what he likes – he will be duly repaid. The passage suggests the difficulty of 'loving your neighbour as yourself', of being tolerant and charitable towards people whom you instinctively dislike, and it introduces *The Friar's Tale* on a note of tense expectation.

The story

A very active summoner, whose job it is to bring offenders to court, is on his way to summon an old widow on a trumped-up charge, when he meets a yeoman. They fall into conversation, the yeoman taking the summoner for a bailiff, and both talking about their work, until eventually the yeoman tells the summoner that he is actually a fiend from hell. The summoner is much interested and likes his companion so well that he gladly agrees to work with him in partnership. As they near the town, they see a carter cursing his horses, and the summoner urges his new friend to take them, but the fiend cannot because, although the carter says one thing, he means another. On they go to the widow's house, where the summoner offensively demands money. He next threatens to take her newest pan instead; but she wishes him and her pan, too, at the devil. Thereupon the fiend asks if she means it, and on hearing that she does, carries off the summoner to hell to satisfy his curiosity about the place. The Friar then concludes his tale with some pious sentiments.

COMMENTARY: No definite source for *The Friar's Tale* is known, though the story itself exists in a number of versions, relating to different professions. Its basis is the popular belief that a curse is effective when it comes from the heart.

Chaucer's version is very well told, but though a satisfying, amusing story, it does not carry deeper meaning. Like the preceding link-passage, it emphasises the difficulty of overcoming hostility and establishing friendly relations with traditional enemies. The Friar savagely denounces summoners, and thus provokes an angry interruption from the Summoner, upon which the Host has to intervene. The exposé of the summoners' activities is resumed by the Friar, who describes them as being like Judas, who betrayed Christ, his master and friend. In this passage (1338–74) the theme of the abuse of friendship and of trust is introduced – a theme which is taken up again in *The Pardoner's Tale* – as the Summoner is described as feigning friendship for those from whom he extorts money.

The story moves forward by means of brilliant passages of dialogue underlaid by irony, as the companions ride on their way. The summoner is ashamed to own to his true occupation and pretends to be a bailiff, unaware that the yeoman knows all about him, and that he has met his match in deceit and unreliability when they swear brotherhood. The tale itself is from the North of England, but the yeoman's claim that his dwelling is 'fer in the north contree' (1413) also alludes to the medieval association of the north with the devil, and his friendly hope of seeing the summoner there can thus be appreciated. The very easy terms on which the two converse adds to the humour: the summoner is not at all put out to find himself in the company of a fiend from hell, and makes the most of his opportunity of satisfying his curiosity about the fiend's way of going about his business. Not only is he perfectly at ease, but the fiend says that he will be better qualified by his own experience for a university chair in the subject of hell and devilry than either Virgil or Dante, who had each written about the infernal world. As they go on their way, the summoner ironically insists on his truth and his sworn brotherhood to his companion, as he is a yeoman (which of course he is not). When they come upon the carter, cursing his horses, the summoner confidentially urges the fiend to take his opportunity, but his simple-minded literalism shows that he is not a match for the devil in his knowledge of human psychology, though he may be in wickedness. The encounter with the old woman makes the same point, for the summoner does not realise that he has chosen the wrong victim when he tries to show off to his companion, telling the fiend to watch how he goes about his business: 'taak heer ensample of me' (1580). His insolent, provocative language fails to intimidate the old woman and he plays into the devil's hands when he says 'the foule feend me fecche/If I th'excuse' (1610–11). Her invocation of God, of 'Crist Jhesu' and of 'Seinte Marie' helps to safeguard her from the powers of evil, and she gives the summoner a chance of escaping damnation if 'he wol hym repente' (1629), but he absolutely refuses to take it, so the fiend takes him, body and soul, together with the old women's pan, as his right. The old woman's sturdy resistance and refusal to be frightened by either summoner or fiend, the realism of her presentation with her sarcastic reply to the summoner's first insult:

"Who clappeth?" seyde this wyf, "*benedicitee*!
God save you sire, what is youre sweete wille?" (1584–5) –

as well as her devil-may-care giving away of her pan, make the ending more effective. The conjunction of the ordinary, everyday world of the widow with the supernatural world of the fiend is piquant. Ironically, though in the real world the summoner fails to achieve his target for the day as well as his boast of extorting twelve pence from the widow, the fiend succeeds in his task. The tale ends appropriately in consequence with a warning to the pilgrims to beware of the devil who 'goeth about as a lion, seeking whom he may devour' (1657).

The Summoner's Prologue and Tale

The Summoner, enraged by *The Friar's Tale*, shakes like a leaf with anger, then begins to revenge himself by speaking of a friar who visits hell in a vision. He sees no friars there and when he inquires whether this is because they are too good for hell, he is shown where they all are: in a vast swarm under the devil's tail. The Summoner then proceeds with his tale, set in Holderness in Yorkshire.

The story

A greedy friar who spends much of his time in highly-organised begging comes to the house of a man whom he has often visited and who is bedridden. He flirts with the wife, gives orders for supper, tells her that he has had a vision of her recently dead child going to heaven, and then goes to give spiritual advice to the husband. The husband complains that all his offerings to the friars in the past have not made their prayers effective in bringing about his recovery; he refuses to confess, so the friar preaches him a long sermon on the sin of anger, and asks for a further donation. The sick man, offering a gift which must be divided equally among all the friars, asks him to put his hand down inside the bed, where he will find a rich gift. When he does so, the patient lets loose a fart, to the fury of the friar who goes to the lord of the village and tells him the tale. The lord and his lady listen sympathetically, but their comment is, What would you expect of a churl but churlish behaviour? As to the problem of how such a gift is to be equally divided, this is ingeniously solved by a young squire, who wins a new gown for his solution.

COMMENTARY: *The Summoner's Tale*, though not one of the most refined, is a superbly told tale in which Chaucer portrays an odious friar with considerable subtlety. The domestic detail, the dialogue and the skill with which Chaucer represents the friar's greed, hypocrisy and sanctimoniousness add to its interest. The tale conjures up a vivid picture of the everyday medieval world and of the professionalism of the mendicant friars, as they go about their work of preying upon ordinary people: meal and cheese, corn and wheat and rye, brawn and bacon and beef as well as money and other goods are collected up and carried off by the friars, who are supposed to be (and claim to be in the tale) vowed to poverty and to have no possessions. The levy is carefully organised and extorted by means of spiritual and emotional blackmail. The visual realism of the narration is continued as the friar arrives at the house of the bed-ridden Thomas, drives the cat off the bench, lays down his stick, his hat and his scrip (alms bag), and makes himself at home, having got rid of his assistant so that he can freely fondle and kiss the wife, flattering her at the same time. He asserts his intention of 'groping the conscience' of the patient, and ironically ends up groping for treasure in the man's bed instead, and getting a not inappropriate reward for the breath expended in his unwanted sermon. The friar is presented as lustful, greedy, boastful and hypocritical. He carefully orders his favourite supper from the sexy wife who encourages him, while he claims that his asceticism leaves him without an appetite. The lively dialogue adds to the realism of the telling: the friar says he wants just the liver of the capon, just a tiny little slice of the wife's bread, and the pig's head, but not, of course, if any animal has to be specially killed for him. We hear the very tones of voice of the unctuous cleric as he appeals to the sick man:

O Thomas, *je vous dy*, Thomas! Thomas!
This maketh the feend; this moste ben amended. (1832–3)

His hypocrisy becomes even more apparent when he pretends to have had a vision of the wife's dead child, 'With many a teere trillyng on my cheke' (1864). The falsely pious discourse (1854–1947) which follows with its allusions to Moses and Elias, to Aaron and to Jesus and to Jovinian (an unorthodox monk (*d. c.*408), whose writings were denounced by St. Jerome) must have been splendidly comic when dramatically read aloud by Chaucer in the appropriately solemn tones of the preacher. In the speech that comes next (1954–2016) he addresses the unfortunate Thomas over and over again by name, to hold his attention and drive home his reproof of Thomas's exasperation and impatience. Meanwhile Chaucer ironically gives a hint of the difficult dilemma with which the tale ends: 'What is a ferthyng worth parted in twelve?' (1967). The sermon with which he continues, (2017–88) contains some good stories: Seneca's tale of the angry potentate who executed three men none of whom were really guilty; Cambises who shot the child of a lord who reproved him for drinking too much, to prove that his steadiness of eye and hand were not impaired; and 'irous Cyrus' who destroyed a river because one of his horses had drowned in it. The sermon also gives an interesting example of medieval preaching techniques: it denounces one of the Seven Deadly Sins, anger, and chooses three examples (which, as is seen here, did not have to be drawn from the Bible) to make the preacher's point. But before boredom can set in, Chaucer reverts to dialogue again with further reiterations of 'Now, Thomas' on the part of the friar, while the enraged sufferer, who is of course unable to get away, naturally has only very limited means of revenge at his disposal. Thomas is in no doubt of the friar's 'dissymulatioun' (2123) and has had enough of it. He has little left to give because of the friar's remorseless exploitation, but gets ready to bestow one last gift, on condition that it shall be fairly divided among all the friars of the 'hooly covent' (2130). The friar gropes, and gets his reward – no cart-horse could have exceeded the blast in magnitude – and he leaps up like an enraged lion, gnashing his teeth like a wild boar, and is appropriately chased away at last by the servants as if he were a savage beast.

A dramatic contrast of tone ensues when the friar goes to the local lord to complain, to be met with the lord's infuriating understatement that 'some thyng ther is amys' (2172). Thomas's unwelcome offering is defined by the pompous friar as blasphemy, 'an odious meschief' which insults the whole of holy church (2190–3), yet again emphasising the friar's self-importance. But the lady of the house, who has heard the tale of woe, comments sensibly: 'a cherl hath doon a cherles dede' (2206), and soothingly dismisses it as a consequence of Thomas's long illness. The lord, meanwhile, who is of a more intellectual cast of mind, is abstractedly puzzling over the problem of how 'arsmetrike' (arithmetic) (2222) can effect a fair division of the unwanted gift. A solution is promptly forthcoming, to round off this elaborate anecdote properly, from the intelligent youth who is doing the carving, and though it is even cruder than the previous joke it is acclaimed as being worthy of Euclid or Ptolemy. It rewards each friar for the 'hot air' of the hypocritical preaching of which his order is deemed to be guilty, with hot air of a kind which indicates the value set upon his words, and appropriately concludes the Summoner's attempt to revenge himself on the Friar.

Chaucer, as also in such tales as the Miller's and Reeve's, pushes his plot to the very limits of plausibility, but the brilliant surface realism which enables us to visualise situations and characters, and the sustained uniformity of tone which binds the various elements together, ensure the tale's success as a work of great technical skill and even of insight into human nature.

The Clerk's Prologue and Tale

When the Host calls on the Clerk to tell a tale, he demands a merry one in a simple unrhetorical style. The Clerk offers to tell one which he had learned, he says, from Petrarch, whose genius had adorned the poetry of

Italy, but he proposes to plunge straight into the story itself, omitting Petrarch's elaborate prologue.

The story

Far away in Italy there lives a young marquis, Walter, who spends his time in heedless pleasure, until one day his people request that he should marry, to provide an heir. He agrees to do so and appoints the day for the wedding. Near his palace is a village in which lives a poor man, Janicula, and his virtuous and beautiful daughter, Griselda. The marquis has seen and admired her, and on the day fixed for the wedding, he rides to her house and asks for her hand in marriage. Her father consents, and after promising the marquis never to disobey him willingly, Griselda becomes his wife.

In due course Griselda has a baby daughter, and then Walter is seized with a desire to test her obedience to the limit. He has her child taken away, saying that it is to be murdered, though in reality he sends it to his sister to be brought up in safety. When later a son is born, he does exactly the same thing as soon as the child reaches the age of two. Each time Griselda submits to Walter's will with patience, but in due course he is urged to test her again. He has their marriage annulled, announces that he wants to marry a younger wife, and sends Griselda back to her father, later summoning her to return to the palace to supervise the arrangements for the wedding. At last, however, his desire to test Griselda is sated. He reveals that the supposed bride is Griselda's daughter, who is accompanied by her little brother. Griselda is reunited with her children; and since Walter's urge to test her is at last satisfied, they live happily ever after.

The story is followed by a song ('Lenvoy de Chaucer') in which the Clerk urges wives to show their spirit and not allow themselves to be treated as Griselda was.

COMMENTARY: *The Clerk's Tale* derives ultimately from a very old folk-tale, which Boccaccio had earlier retold as the last of the tales in his *Decameron*, and which Petrarch in turn had translated into Latin. Chaucer based his version on Petrarch's, though he also used a French translation of the Italian, by an anonymous author. The story was already very popular when Chaucer came across it. In its earliest form it was a folk-tale about the mating of a mortal woman with an immortal man. It follows typical folk-tale patterns in other ways, too: the rags-to-riches motif, the triple testing and the happy ending. Problems are created for the modern reader because Chaucer's retelling enhances the human interest and makes it not just a simple folk-tale, but a story of deeper meaning, in reading which our sympathies are more closely involved with the heroine than is entirely comfortable. In our modern literal-mindedness, moreover, we may be tempted to read the tale as an account of a real-life marriage, but as with Shakespeare's treatment of obsessive jealousy in *The Winter's Tale*, we should not expect full motivation or psychological realism. *The Clerk's Tale* is a tale of far away and long ago, which raises questions about human behaviour in general terms; not about real people, but about a situation and a terrible trial and the triumph of the human spirit that finally overcomes evil. Walter's desire to prove his wife is so cruel and obsessive that it dehumanises him, while Griselda is like the patient, good girls in folk-tales (as in the Russian tale, *King Frost*), whose steadfastness turns mindless evil into good. We are shown that a human being can be tried to the utmost limits of endurance – Griselda has to bear the greatest suffering that a mother can undergo – and can emerge victorious in the end.

In *The Clerk's Tale* we have in Walter a typical character from traditional story – the cruel, dominant male – while in Griselda we have the weak and helpless victim who overcomes in the end. Such victories result from superiority other than that of physical strength, from superior goodness or intelligence or love. Walter, presented as a powerful medieval overlord, is not accountable to anyone. Though he is prepared to marry to please his subjects and to provide an heir, he expects full obedience from them. His mode of choosing his bride – 'this povre creature' (232) whom he has chanced to see while out hunting – is capricious, while the offer of his subjects to choose a bride for him and his own method of selection emphasise the impersonal nature of the marriage relationship and the folk-tale aspects of the story.

Griselda conforms to medieval ideals of goodness and simplicity, her constancy contrasted to the fickleness of the 'people'. She is the type of patient endurance, as Walter is the type of the ruthless tyrant. Against the senseless cruelty of Walter's treatment of her, her fortitude is rocklike; nothing that he can devise to torment her can break her spirit.

The Clerk's Tale is based on the concept upon which the meaning of *Troilus and Criseyde* and *The Franklin's Tale* turns; 'trouthe'. It is Troilus's 'trouthe' which, as his dominant characteristic, keeps him faithful to Criseyde despite her treachery. Arveragus and Dorigen in *The Franklin's Tale* acknowledge that a promise must be kept, no matter what the consequences, if the individual is to be true to him or herself. Such 'trouthe' is the integrity on which self-respect depends, and without which there can be no trust among human beings. Griselda's constancy is a subtle version of this same quality, for we see that she is true to her promise of obedience, freely made to Walter before her marriage, because only in this way can she be true to herself. The firmness with which she holds on to an abstract ideal shows that her patience and constancy are more than mere passive acceptance of the worst that life can bring to her.

Walter is also to be seen as an instrument of Fortune, the means by which, ultimately under providence, Griselda is to be tested to the limit. Chaucer places some emphasis on the concept of Fortune: in lines 754-6, we are told that Griselda is resolutely disposed to endure the 'adversitee of Fortune', and Walter, in sending her back to her father, advises her to endure the 'strook of Fortune' with an 'evene herte' (811-2). The people who follow her, as she returns barefoot to her father's house, curse Fortune on her behalf as they go (897-8). All human beings have to endure misfortune as best they can, but Griselda never loses her self-command or her dignity; and her surrender of her 'wyl' and 'libertee' to Walter at her marriage never deprives her of her inner freedom or her integrity.

Walter, meanwhile, is enslaved to his own evil obsession – his desire to test his wife – which drives him on to increasingly outrageous acts. He is not satisfied with her promise of obedience. At first, when before their marriage Griselda swears that she will never willingly disobey him, 'In werk ne thoght' (363), he is content: 'This is ynogh, Grisilde myn' (365) he says. But it soon ceases to be enough to satisfy him and his desire to prove her becomes insatiable. Before ever the first child is taken from her, we are told that Walter has 'assayed hire ynogh bifore' (456). Thus the story turns upon the idea of 'enough', and the extent to which Walter's greedy desire to test Griselda is matched and eventually overcome by the even greater patience which enables her to endure the trials he devises.

In a sense, it is Walter who suffers, the victim of a totally irrational and uncontrollable urge to torment. Griselda's patience is the fruit of a love which ultimately redeems him, to the point at which he can finally say, once more, 'This is ynogh, Grisilde myn' (1051), and mean it. Her constancy enables her, not merely to survive but to so satisfy Walter that their story can ultimately resolve itself in 'concorde and in reste', 'in pees and reste', and finally 'In reste and pees' (1128-36) for them both.

Griselda remains, through all that Walter can inflict upon her, 'sad', a word by which Chaucer means, not melancholy or unhappy, but steadfast, firm, or constant. She is 'so stidefast' (564); 'evere in oon ylike sad and kynde' (602); 'ay sad and constant as a wal' (1047), contrasting in her unchangeable 'stedfastnesse' and 'sadness' with Walter's people, who are described as being 'unsad and evere untrewe' (995). The word 'sad' had earlier carried the meaning of 'satisfied'; and in this tale we see that Griselda's constancy, arising from her love, leads at last to the satisfaction of her love in Walter's eventual change of heart, and to his satisfaction, too.

Such steadfastness cannot be achieved without immense cost. The extent to which Griselda has suffered is indicated when, reunited with her children 'Al sodeynly she swapte adoun to grounde' (1099), clasping her children in her arms 'so sadly' that it is only with great difficulty that they can be released from their unconscious mother's embrace. But though Griselda appears to be the passive victim of Walter's monstrous designs, she in fact manifests a positive energy from beginning to end. She is always in command of the situation; neither the 'ugly sergeant' who is sent to take her children from her, nor Walter himself can break her spirit. At the third test, for example, this is her response to her husband:

'I have,' quod she, 'seyd thus, and evere shal:
I wol no thyng, ne nyl no thyng, certayn,
But as yow list. Naught greveth me at al . . . ' (645–7)

In her submission, she can even command her oppressor:

Ye been oure lord, dooth with youre owene thyng
Right as yow list; axeth no reed at me. (652–3)

It is this very positiveness that may make it difficult for the modern reader to appreciate the tale to the full. Chaucer makes Griselda come alive to such an extent that we may become emotionally involved to an uncomfortable extent. Instead of telling the story of Griselda in the simple straightforward manner of folk-tale, Chaucer allows the characters to speak for themselves, and lively dialogue, such as that quoted above, sometimes gives them an unexpected measure of psychological realism, while their situation remains unrealistic. In consequence, Walter's behaviour seems even more intolerable and outrageous, and Griselda's acceptance of it more incomprehensible.

The teller of the tale also directly involves the reader's response. His voice of reason and sympathy puts the story that he is telling in a human perspective. Contrary to what one would expect from a clerk, he is very sympathetic to women, praising their humility and faithfulness (936–8). From the very beginning, he comments personally on the action, saying of Walter, for example, 'I blame hym thus' (78), and later asking why he needed to continue to test Griselda 'alwey moore and moore' when there was no need (458). He leaves us in no doubt that Walter's behaviour is to be regarded as evil, deriving from a 'crueel purpos' (740), as we see from the reaction of the people, who believe that he has wickedly, secretly murdered his children from a 'crueel herte' (722–6).

In other ways, too, the liveliness of Chaucer's narration makes for tension between the highly improbable plot and the realism that brings the story to life: the vivid little sketches, such as that of Griselda contriving to fetch water so as to see the marquis pass her house; and of Walter's feigned look of displeasure, despite his real satisfaction, as he leaves Griselda's room (512–5). Later, in another realistic passage, Griselda directs the servants and sees to the sweeping, setting the tables and making the beds, to prepare the palace for the new bride. The pathos of her situation is thus even more strongly and painfully brought out.

Though *The Clerk's Tale* was once considered an answer to the Wife of Bath's views on marriage, it is not primarily about marriage at all, but about integrity and the redemptive power of steadfast love. It is not significant that in realistic terms it seems a preposterous story, for it is not what actually happens in it that matters. The poem is a celebration of the triumph of the human spirit over the worst that can befall it, and of the unfaltering love that enables Griselda to endure torment and, in a sense, to redeem her husband. The story was sometimes interpreted as an allegory of the Christian soul's relationship with God (Walter thus representing God), to emphasise the need for patience and obedience to His will. Chaucer's retelling reverses the roles of Walter and Griselda, so that new meanings emerge. The emphasis falls, not on the harshness of the demands that God makes upon the faithful soul, but on the power of unfailing love and patience to redeem. In this respect, Griselda's love for Walter is truly Christlike.

The Merchant's Prologue and Tale

The Merchant and the Host commiserate with each other over their sufferings as married men, and then the Merchant begins his tale of January and May.

The story

In times long past there is an old bachelor knight who suddenly decides that he wishes to be married before he dies on the grounds that a wife is God's gift and it is a wonderful thing to have one. So the knight, January, tells his friends Placebo and Justinus of his desire and says that he must have a very young wife. Placebo supports his intention, while Justinus points out the difficulties. However January persists and eventually selects the beautiful young May. They are married and at last January is able to go to bed with May, but his young squire, Damian, is already sick with love for her. When the unsuspecting January urges May to visit Damian, who is ill in bed, the squire contrives to slip her a letter, but she is so closely guarded by her jealous husband that no further progress in the affair can be made. Sometime later, January goes blind, but he keeps hold of May all the time and often makes love to her in his private garden. At last May gets a spare key and gives it to Damian, making an assignation with him. But Pluto, King of Fairyland, is in the garden, sees what May and Damian intend to do, and declares that he will give January back his sight. Pluto's wife, Proserpine, objects, and says that, as compensation, she will give May and all women for ever after the gift of finding a plausible explanation. Damian climbs into a pear tree, and May joins him. Just when Damian is in the act of making love, January's sight is restored. His roars of jealous rage are soothed by May, who explains that she has only acted in this way to restore his sight; furthermore, she tells him that he did not see what he thought he saw because he had not quite regained his sight. So January becomes a happy man again.

COMMENTARY: *The Merchant's Tale* is January's story, despite the participation in it of the three pairs of characters, Placebo and Justinus, May and Damian, Pluto and Proserpine. It is a story on the theme of human blindness, a tale which makes no attempt to be realistic. Its ironies, ambiguities and frequently shifting tone and point of view emphasise our readiness to deceive ourselves, to believe what we want to believe, to resist enlightenment and to prefer self-deception when the truth is unpalatable. January's perverse refusal to 'see' the folly of his plan for marriage later turns to literal blindness in physical terms, but when his sight returns, he still rejects what he has seen, to return to his fool's paradise. The 'paradise' of his married state is as much a mockery of true paradise as his private garden is of the biblical paradise it invokes. (Indeed, one could say that Adam's disobedience, which cost him his paradise, is paralleled by January's disobedience to the dictates of reason.) In *The Merchant's Tale* Chaucer makes use of traditional material concerning marriage, already drawn on for *The Wife of Bath's Prologue*, and he combines it with the pear-tree episode, a well-known motif in folk-lore. Characteristically, the tale shows Chaucer's disapproval of marriages in which there was great disparity of age, and his sympathetic attitude to women. The story divides itself into several separate parts, each one enriched with reference and allusions, but for a number of reasons it is not entirely a success from an artistic point of view.

In the first part of the tale, January's persistent folly in insisting that at the age of sixty, after a life of lechery, it is time to marry, is followed by a long, sharply ironic passage about the excellence of the married state. Traditional misogynistic writing supplies much of the substance of the passage, which further indirectly indicates January's folly: he is silly enough actually to *believe* such pronouncements as 'How myghte a man han any adversitee/That hath a wyf?' (1338–9). Though we are not told whether it is the Merchant (unhappily married himself) who utters the ironic comments on marriage, the implication and the joke is that January really accepts all these assertions as true.

January's insistence on marrying, though he recognises that he is on the brink of his grave, leads on to the entrance of his two advisers, one the courtly flatterer, the other the voice of prudence and commonsense. This is, we realise, a schematic rather than a realistic tale, in which issues will be simplified and situations presented in general terms, although Chaucer enhances the narrative with dramatic tension. January makes himself ridiculous with his sexual boasting and naive enthusiasm, Placebo's grave approval shows up the hypocrisy of flatterers, and Justinus's commonsense is of course rejected out of hand. The humour, however, has a bitter quality throughout the tale, deriving from the sharpness of the irony, for January's sexual fantasising – leading to his fear that he will miss heaven in the end because he has had it on earth – and Justinus's warning imply that marriage cannot in any circumstances be heaven on earth. The bitterness of the tale is further emphasised by the ending: January regains his sight and continues to possess his beautiful young wife, so that he retains all that he had originally wanted, while there can be no happiness for May. But the tale must be read as a tale about human folly, rather than as a tale about love, or as a serious contribution to a 'marriage debate'. Though many of *The Canterbury Tales* are concerned with marriage in one way or another, they are not primarily intended to constitute a discussion of marriage as an institution, as was once thought. We might note here, however, that we have an indication in *The Merchant's Tale* that Chaucer envisaged *The Canterbury Tales* as a unified whole rather than as a mere collection of disparate stories. This is to be found in the rather surrealistic reference to the Wife of Bath in the tale. It is not simply that the Merchant refers to the Wife as an authority on marriage, but rather the fact that the fictional character of Justinus says that the Wife 'Declared hath ful wel in litel space' (1687), on the subject under discussion.

When the discussion of pros and cons is completed and the marriage of January and May takes place, Chaucer blends classical and biblical reference both to dignify the full description of their wedding and to intensify the absurdity of January's pretensions to be a great lover, as he longs to clasp May in his arms, 'Harder than evere Parys dide Eleyne' (1754). Romance soon shifts to harsh realism as January drinks aphrodisiacs, and kisses

> His fresshe May, his paradys, his make . . .
> With thikke brustles of his berd unsofte
> Lyk to the skyn of houndfyssh, sharp as brere –
> For he was shave al newe in his manere – (1822–6)

pretending to look like a beardless boy. There is a peculiar nastiness in the forced love-making of the old lecher, a quality which distinguishes this tale from the hearty sexuality of Chaucer's other *fabliaux*, such as the Miller's and Reeve's tales.

The squire Damian meanwhile languishes in the pains of 'courtly' love. Almost driven mad with longing, and almost swooning, he has seen May married to his master and has taken to his bed, weeping and lamenting. He shows the classic symptoms of more noble lovers such as Troilus, but the fate of his love-letter privily read and disposed of by the practical May, makes the furtive, sordid nature of the affair appropriate to the participants in it. Chaucer's comment on May's pity for Damian's distress 'Lo, pitee renneth soone in gentil herte!' (1986) ironically echoes line 1761 in *The Knight's Tale* and suggests the diversity of human nature. May's pity, unlike that of Duke Theseus, is not without self-interest; Damian suffers – as do Palamon and Arcite – according to his nature, but that he is servile is made clear by the comment:

And eek to Januarie he gooth as lowe
As evere dide a dogge for the bowe. (2013–4)

The next part of the tale brings in a new element, as Chaucer describes in parodic terms the garden to which January likes to go with May. He says it is like the garden in the *Roman de la Rose*, a romantic place for lovers to meet, securely walled so as to keep out all that is hostile to love; and so beautiful that even Priapus, the 'god of gardyns' (2035) could not describe it adequately. The mention of Priapus, the monstrous mythological figure with grossly disproportionate sexual organs who is alluded to in *The Parliament of Fowls*, helps to set the tone for the passage, for here we are told of January's love-making on 'many a murye day' (2053), even after he is struck blind by adverse fortune. January's 'olde lewed wordes' (2149) to May parody not medieval romance but *The Song of Solomon*, 'the song of songs', in the Bible. This book, now usually thought to be a secular love song, was interpreted allegorically in Chaucer's day as a description of God's dealings with the Church or with the individual soul. January's distortion of it is grotesque, and followed by an equally strange passage, in which January speaks in very serious terms of his love for May, and she, gesticulating meanwhile to Damian who is in the garden too, utters conventional sentiments about her soul, her honour, and her intention to be true. 'I am a gentil womman and no wenche' (2202) she asserts; but nothing in this tale can be taken at its face value.

Brightly the sun shines, while the human beings plan deception; and meanwhile the king and queen of Fairyland have come to the garden too. Pluto brings with him more than a hint of the sinister. In classical mythology he was king of the underworld, and Chaucer alludes to the story of how he had carried off Proserpine to his dark kingdom in his 'grisely carte' (2233), his act of taking possession of his beautiful bride paralleling January's of May. The antagonism between men and women to which the earlier part of the tale indirectly and ironically alluded (1267–1392), and which Justinus had also suggested (1521–66 and 1659–84), is paralleled by the antagonism between Pluto and

Proserpine. Even the dark, subterranean powers are at odds; hostility between male and female seems to be a law of nature; their purposes and their interests seem, in this harsh tale, to be in perpetual conflict. There is comedy, however, in the situation itself, in the unknown presence of the fairies in the garden and in their commentary on human behaviour, their partisanship and their own individual conflict, which makes them determined to counter each other's intentions. (They are, of course, to be thought of as supernatural beings on a human scale, rather than as the pretty little fairies of more recent folk-lore). There is comedy also, in the ability of Pluto and Proserpine to allude to scripture and make other learned references; as well as in Proserpine's determination to give all women, for ever after, the power to talk themselves out of difficult situations. This passage also usefully reminds us that this tale of far away and long ago, despite some surface realism which allows fleeting glimpses of what seems a real-life situation, is not a tale about real people at all, but about how human beings in general may be foolish enough to behave.

The narration shifts for the last part of the tale (2320 to the end) to a more dramatic and fast-moving mode. January sings of love more merrily than a parrot (2322), May pretends that she is pregnant and has a craving for pears, and makes her husband help her up into the tree where the athletic Damian already awaits her. The story-teller is coy, at first, about what Damian actually does, though leaving the reader in no doubt: 'Ladyes, I prey yow that ye be nat wrooth' (2350), and then dramatically, at the crucial moment, January's sight is restored and he 'yaf a roryng and a cry,/As dooth the mooder whan the child shal dye' (2364–5). May is ready with the explanation and January eventually has to accept it. Pluto enables him to see both literally and also metaphorically, in that he realises what is actually going on: then he relapses into psychological blindness again. He believes May; he rejects the evidence of his senses, preferring self-deception.

The Merchant's Tale thus skilfully blends many different elements, combining traditional lore and learning, classical mythology and biblical reference, argument and straightforward narrative. Literary parody is balanced by the knock-about comedy of *fabliau*. Lively dialogue brings about the swift well-managed dénouement and the pear-tree episode is enhanced by Chaucer's intriguing addition of the gifts of the fairies. These gifts have the effect of both making the ending more dramatic, and of intensifying the meaning, as January chooses not to confront the truth. But the tone of the poem is not simply pervasively ironic, it is also consistently bitter: men, young and old, are all lechers (1249, 2257); men and women constantly deceive each other. May asserts that 'men been evere untrewe' (2203) when she is on the brink of being untrue herself, while Pluto who has carried off Proserpine and forced her to become his bride speaks of 'The tresons whiche that wommen doon to man' (2239).

The tale is followed by a brief epilogue in which the Host complains about his wife and her faults, but sensibly declares 'Therof no fors! lat alle swiche thynges go' (2430). This is good advice for the reader: we must accept the Merchant's jaundiced view of married life and of the blindness of human beings as a valid one, but it is only one view after all. It is counter-balanced by *The Franklin's Tale*, for example, which Chaucer probably intended to place after it.

The Squire's Introduction and Tale

It is by no means certain which pilgrim Chaucer chose to tell the next tale, but scholars have placed *The Squire's Tale* (which is unfinished) after the Merchant's, with which it strongly contrasts.

The form of *The Canterbury Tales* enabled Chaucer to experiment with many different kinds of story and *The Squire's Tale* is an example of a medieval romance. As such, it has something in common with romances of later periods, and even of the present day, but it was a mode which did not suit Chaucer's genius as well as more realistic types of story, and he abandoned this tale long before the end. When the turn of Chaucer the pilgrim comes later on, he tells the story of Sir Thopas, which brilliantly makes fun of the absurdities of the hackneyed medieval romance of his day, and this (though the Host does not appreciate his contribution) is much more subtle and successful than *The Squire's Tale*.

The story

In the land of Tartary there is a noble king, Cambyuskan, who has two sons and a beautiful daughter called Candace. At one of his great feasts, a strange knight appears riding a horse of brass and bringing a mirror, a ring and a sword. They are presents: the horse can fly anywhere in the world in the course of a day; the mirror warns of coming misfortune and also allows one to distinguish friend from foe; the ring offers the power to understand the language of the birds; the sword inflicts a wound that can only be cured by the application of the same sword. The crowds of onlookers view the horse with suspicion and marvel at the other presents. The knight shows how the horse is operated and the celebration continues. In the morning Candace is up early and goes out for a walk, during which she sees a falcon and is enabled by her ring to understand its speech. The falcon is heart-broken because she has been deserted by her lover, so Candace takes the poor bird back to the palace. The Squire then mentions the stories to follow about Cambyuscan and his family, but the tale is broken off after only two lines of Part 3.

COMMENTARY: *The Squire's Tale* has considerable charm as an example of romance, but like romances then and now, the story is filled out with a great deal of detail. We see a typical medieval feast, for example, in the description of Cambyuskan's anniversary celebration: his royal state, the magnificent dishes, the delicious music, the strange knight's arrival, upon which the whole hall falls silent. *The Squire's Tale* is a typical romance also in that it involves some significant objects with magical powers: the horse, mirror, ring and sword, though it is only the virtue of the ring that is demonstrated. Its characters are also exceptional: it is about a king and his lovely and virtuous daughter, though we see something of the 'lewed people' (for example, in 221) who are suspicious of the brazen horse. The unhappy falcon who speaks of her betrayal brings in the theme of magic, and, being noble, is an exceptional figure, but she also brings in a characteristic romance element, that of love. We can see that, as in many other such stories, the adventures and incidents could go on virtually for ever, if we were allowed a full account of Cambyuscan, Algarsif, Candace and all the other characters involved, but probably Chaucer found that the narrative lacked human interest, and that he did not wish to spin an endless yarn, consisting merely of adventure after adventure. Clearly the fact that a principal character was not a true human being but a bird imposed a limitation upon the story's potential for psychological realism.

Love

The tale is interesting for the extent to which it gives insight into fourteenth-century love conventions. The falcon is loved by a tercelet who seems all that the ideal lover should be – 'welle of alle gentilesse' (505), humble and apparently true. He offers his service to his love, performing his 'cerymonyes and obeisaunces', and all his observances as a lover should (515-6), and they exchange hearts (535). The relationship develops further, in that the falcon submits to the will of the tercelet in everything, 'as fer as reson fil,/Kepynge the boundes of my worshipus evere' (571-2), and their love-affair continues for a long time. Separation makes them both miserable, when the tercelet has to leave 'For his honour' (592), like Arveragus in *The Franklin's Tale*. But at once all his vows are forgotten, for he is distracted by another bird and deserts his love. After this act of betrayal, the falcon sees all the former devotion of the tercelet as mere hypocrisy. The 'gentil ... fressh and gay ... goodlich ... humble and free' (622-3) tercelet has become 'this god of loves ypocryte' (514).

Just as earlier in *The Book of the Duchess*, Chaucer had given an account of the joys and sorrows of a male lover, deprived of his beloved by her untimely death, here he gives us a somewhat similar situation from the woman's point of view. Chaucer shows that the same intensity of feeling is involved on the woman's side as on the man's; indeed, the falcon in her anguish has so torn her breast with her beak that she is almost at the point of death. Chaucer does not describe, as he does with Troilus (in *Troilus and Criseyde*), the physical sufferings of the early stages of love, because they were part of the male, not the female, lover's experience, but here, as often elsewhere in medieval literature, we see that love inevitably involves suffering, whatever the relationship.

Narrative technique and rhetoric

The *Squire's Tale* contains a number of references to the technique of story-telling, very typical of Chaucer. After the 'once upon a time' beginning, Chaucer (in the person of the Squire) says that his English is insufficient to describe the beauty of Candace. This is the conventional modesty of the medieval story-teller, but it is particularly appropriate to this tale. Chaucer made no such disclaimer in *The Miller's Tale*, where he gives a very comprehensive account of the charms of his heroine, but here he is speaking of the ideal, out-of-this-world heroine of romance, to whom it is almost impossible to do justice. Similarly, he says that he cannot give an adequate account of what the strange knight on the brazen horse actually said. References to the Arthurian legend – to 'Gawayn, with his olde curtesye' (95) and to Launcelot (287) – remind us of the general context of this story, the ideal world of romance, which is distanced from the everyday world of ordinary experience, but which gives us a different perspective on it. The tone is remarkably consistent throughout this story, and Chaucer makes use of conventional devices to keep it so. He uses *occupatio* to indicate the superlative nature of the arrangements, saying that he will not tell of the wonderful dishes at the feast (67); and he later declares that there is no need to describe everything in detail (298) for it can be left to the reader's imagination, just as he says he will not unduly prolong the description of Candace's walk, for fear of being tedious. He adorns the story with rhetorical flourishes such as that at the beginning of the second part, when the courtly company fall asleep, a device which has its counterpart in the cinema when transitions are marked by atmospheric or scenic shots.

No definite source is known for this tale, for which Chaucer seems to have brought together a variety of elements. It appears to have been a comparatively late work, but by the time that he wrote it, Chaucer must have been coming to realise that pure romance was the wrong mode for his genius.

The Franklin's Prologue and Tale

As the Squire ends his tale, the Franklin congratulates him on it, and says that he wishes that his son were more like the young Squire, and endowed with the quality of 'gentilesse' (discussed in *The Wife of Bath's Tale*). The Host expresses his contempt for 'gentilesse', but begs the Franklin to tell his story, which turns out to be partly concerned with the same theme.

In his prologue the Franklin says that he will tell a Breton lay, but the audience must excuse the plainness of his telling, for he has never learnt the techniques of professional story-tellers. A Breton lay was a short, romantic narrative poem, of a kind composed by Marie de France in the late twelfth century, probably from stories of Celtic origin. (In fact Chaucer seems to have taken the story from Boccaccio, who tells it twice.)

The story

The story tells of a certain knight in Brittany who, newly married to his beloved Dorigen, has agreed with her that he will only assume the outward form of authority over her, so that they will really be equal partners in marriage. After a time, he has to go to England to gain honour by means of knightly deeds, leaving Dorigen behind. She is grief-striken without him, and becomes obsessed by the threat to his safe return presented by the rocks along the coastline. A young squire, Aurelius, meanwhile falls in love with her, and Dorigen foolishly, in an unguarded moment, agrees that she will give him her love if he can remove the rocks from the coast. Her husband Arveragus, however, arrives home safely in due course. Aurelius, still tormented with love for Dorigen, meets a clever young clerk, or scholar, who is able to perform works of magic; and for an enormous sum of money, he agrees to remove the rocks. The rocks duly vanish and Aurelius comes to Dorigen to claim her love. Arveragus is temporarily away; in his absence Dorigen becomes distraught and contemplates suicide. When he returns, she tells him of her dreadful plight and he replies that there is nothing for it but for her to keep her promise to Aurelius, since truth to one's word matters more than anything else. When Aurelius sees her distress, he cannot bring himself to claim her. When he asks the magician to give him time to pay, the magician waives his claim to the money, and the story ends by asking who is the most generous – Arveragus, Aurelius, or the magician?

COMMENTARY: *The Franklin's Tale* is one of the most delightful and moving of Chaucer's tales. The mutual love between Arveragus and Dorigen, which causes them to enter into what was, for the time, an unusual relationship, motivates Dorigen's grief when his career calls Arveragus away, her distress when her foolish promise is unexpectedly claimed, and Arveragus' anguish when his integrity forces him to surrender his wife, as it seems, to Aurelius. Though the tale nowhere suggests that the arrangement entered into by Arveragus and Dorigen is ideal, or constitutes a pattern to be followed, it does define the qualities necessary for happy marriage. The first of these qualities is, of course, love, freely given (764–7); but patience is necessary, as well, as Chaucer points out (773) and emphasises when he says 'Lerneth to suffre' (learn to endure) (777).

Patience and 'trouthe'

It is Dorigen's lack of patience that brings her troubles upon her. Also essential for happy marriage is mutual trust; and we see that Dorigen is at last forced to confide her trouble to her husband, let him decide what should be done, and take responsibility. Arveragus had gone overseas to seek the honour, fame and public recognition that are accorded to noble deeds of chivalry, for he is a knight. But when he returns home and Dorigen tells him of her dire trouble, he is presented with a dilemma that threatens honour. He can either refuse to allow Dorigen to fulfil her foolish promise to Aurelius, or he can destroy his reputation by allowing himself to be cuckolded. He recognises that promises must be kept in a civilised society: 'Trouthe is the hyeste thyng that man may kepe' (1479), and so more important than anything else. Arveragus values personal integrity, the knowledge that he is true to his word, above other qualities; and he and Dorigen, as man and wife, are one flesh, so that her word is his word. His integrity is more important to him than what people may say about him. Truth, one of God's attributes, was particularly highly valued in the fourteenth century (as Chaucer's *Troilus and Criseyde* makes clear) and the theme of keeping promises is a recurrent one in the literature of the time. Only on a foundation of love, patience and truth, or integrity, can firm and lasting relationships, private or public, be built. In this tale, we see that when Arveragus decides that Dorigen must keep her promise, in the end the effect is not negative and destructive, but positive and creative. Arveragus's 'grete gentilesse' (1527) inspires Aurelius to equal (or almost equal) generosity and Aurelius's determination to keep his 'trouthe' (1570 and 1577) moves the learned scholar to release him from his obligation. Aurelius explains, in words which sum up the situation:

Arveragus, of gentillesse,
Hadde levere dye in sorwe and in distresse
Than that his wyf were of hir trouthe fals (1595–7)

and he continues

> That made me han of hire so greet pitee;
> And right as frely as he sente hire me,
> As frely sente I hire to hym ageyn. (1603–5)

The patience which Chaucer mentions early in the tale is a key concept for appreciating the unfolding of the story. Medieval Christianity stressed the importance of patience. It implied the acceptance of whatever God sent, in the belief that it was ultimately for the best. God's loving providence must be trusted, and suffering seen as for the soul's good. Dorigen, however, is unable to accept that the presence of the 'grisly rokkes blake' (859) near the coast of Brittany is for the best. In a long complaint (865–93) she reproves God for allowing the rocks to be there and even asks Him, 'Why han ye wroght this werk unresonable?' (872) showing her lack of patience. When at last the rocks disappear, we can see how interference with God's arrangements can do more harm than good, for the rocks do not cease to exist, they only cease to be visible, thus presumably constituting an even greater danger than when they could be seen. Fortunately for Arveragus, God's 'purveiaunce' or providence has seen to it that the rocks only disappear long after he has safely returned home.

Love

Love is seen in different guises in *The Franklin's Tale*. Arveragus, in accordance with convention, has suffered 'wo, peyne and ... distresse' (737) before winning Dorigen as his wife. She has taken Arveragus both as her 'servant and hir lord' (792). He has unconventionally promised to obey her as if he was still her lover, and he has agreed not to force her to do anything against her will. When he goes to England, she is inconsolable, though her friends do their best to cheer her, and her anxiety about the rocks further shows the strength of her love for her husband. Then Aurelius comes upon the scene, loving Dorigen without daring to tell her for two years and more (940). When Dorigen at last hears his piteous plea for mercy, she assures him that she will never be an untrue wife (984); but then is foolish enough, because of her obsession with the rocks, to say that she will love him if he removes them all. Of course she can no more really give him her love, when the rocks disappear from sight, than he can actually get rid of the rocks. Their seeming absence could only be rewarded, at best, by the semblance of love, in the form of Dorigen's unwilling compliance with Aurelius's desire. The interview between them ends with a firm assurance from Dorigen that there is no sense in his loving 'another mannes wyf' (1004); and the suffering of the unfortunate young man, who, two years later, is still 'in langour and in torment furyus' (1101), completely incapacitated by his misplaced infatuation, is only intensified. His heart is pierced by the 'arwe kene' (1112) of love. When at last the rocks seem to have disappeared, Chaucer makes it very clear that they only seem to have gone (1296), but Aurelius has fulfilled Dorigen's condition and he greets his sovereign lady humbly and anxiously as a lover should (1309–10), reminding her of her promise. He insists that he will die (1315–17), that she will heartlessly kill him (1318–19) if she breaks her 'trouthe' (1320), emphasising that she had pledged her 'trouthe' to love him best (1328–9), and insisting finally that his life is in her hands (1336–7). The febrile intensity of medieval love can lead to a mature relationship of mutual trust, but it can only find proper fulfilment in marriage, and Aurelius's misplaced passion can only end in misery. Dorigen's horrified comment on the disappearance of the rocks, 'It is agayns the proces of nature' (1345), applies indirectly to what is now asked of her: that she should love Aurelius best, but he too has to learn that he demanded the impossible, and to come to terms with the fact, for 'Love wol nat been constreyned by maistrye' (764). Chaucer eventually shows us as near perfect a marriage relationship as human beings can achieve when, all trials past, Arveragus and Dorigen 'In sovereyn blisse leden forth hir lyf' (1552), he cherishing her as if she were a queen, and she being always true to him, in mutual love that can find no place for anger (1553–5).

Astrology and magic

The astrological details of the process by which the rocks are made to disappear are not easy to understand nowadays; and indeed Chaucer emphasises that the 'magyk natureel', in which the clerk of Orleans was so skilled, belonged to a former age and 'in oure dayes is nat worth a flye' (1132). Furthermore, 'swiche illusiouns and swiche meschaunces/As hethen folk useden in thilke days' (1293–3) are no longer fully comprehensible to the Franklin, so the modern reader need not puzzle long over the 'tables Tolletanes' and the other technicalities by means of which the wonder comes to pass; they all make the process suitably complicated and mysterious, and we are not meant to follow in detail. That it is all illusion is made clear from the start: Aurelius's helpful brother asserts that there are sciences that can bring about 'diverse appearances' (1140), which seem to everyone to be real (1151), and extends the application of these arts to the problem of the rocks (1157–9). The 'subtil clerk' encourages Aurelius to believe that he will be able to 'maken illusioun' by 'apparence or jogelrye' (1264–5) that the rocks have gone. Probably the clerk was able to calculate when there would be exceptionally high spring tides which would be likely to cover the rocks temporarily, thus bringing about the desired illusion. 'Magyk natureel', or white magic, was an acceptable 'science' in the Middle Ages, since it was thought to operate by natural means, whereas black magic was condemned by the Church because it involved conjuring up the devil and evil spirits.

The clerk of Orleans's powers are not only demonstrated when the rocks disappear, but earlier, too, when Aurelius first visits him. Before supper, the clerk shows him scenes in which deer are killed by hounds, herons slain by hawks, and in which knights joust; then he sees a vision of himself dancing with his beloved lady. Finally the clerk claps his hands, and it all vanishes, after a convincing demonstration of his remarkable powers. The images that Aurelius sees, however, also enrich the poem by giving in a rather surrealistic way a sense of what is going on in his own mind: his anguished longing for Dorigen can be envisaged in terms of fierce animal aggression, fading to the less savage conflict of two knights, perhaps representing Arveragus and himself, and finally to the vision of his 'dance of love' with Dorigen.

Narrative technique

Chaucer's insight into human nature is made apparent by such means as Aurelius's vision. The story, ostensibly set in far away, long-ago Brittany, is not of course meant to be totally realistic, but it is true to life at a deeper level and its moral seriousness is accompanied by sympathy – particularly for Dorigen – and humour. Such a story does not require naturalistic characterisation: Arveragus is the type of the noble husband, Aurelius the type of the rival lover, and his brother and the clerk of Orleans are merely characters demanded by the plot. Dorigen, the foolish young wife, is not merely a stock figure but is poignantly individualised. Her anxiety for her husband's safety, expressing itself in her indignation at the 'unreasonableness' of God, and her foolish promise to Aurelius in an unguarded moment 'in pley' (988), makes her very human. She does not expect to be taken at her word and the folk-tale motif of the foolish promise is made realistic by her assertions before and after it: she assures Aurelius that she will never be an untrue wife, and urges him to dismiss his foolish hopes. Her love for her husband finds expression in the physical satisfaction of having him in her arms again when at last he returns home. But when he has to go away again, and the full horror of Aurelius's expectations dawns upon Dorigen, she utters a long 'compleynt' (1355–1456) which because it is so stylised, modern readers may find hard to appreciate. As a story-telling device, however, it works well, firstly because it places Dorigen's plight in a context of similar situations: should she – will she – choose to die as other unfortunate wives have done in the past? Secondly, it works well because the passage is not without psychological realism. In such a situation, it is natural to think of others who have had the same problem, and in calling to mind every similar case, Dorigen begins to work off the first hysterical promptings of despair, until eventually, instead of killing herself, she decides to tell her husband. The ensuing scene between them contrasts sharply with her solitary 'compleynt' in its dramatic terseness and naturalistic dialogue. Arveragus asks, in 'freendly wyse',

> 'Is ther oght elles, Dorigen, but this?'
> 'Nay, nay,' quod she, 'God helpe me so as wys!
> This is to muche, and it were Goddes wille.' (1469–71)

The calm strength of his unhesitating integrity tells her at once what she must do; but the real depth of his feeling is shown when he immediately 'brast anon to wepe' (1480). Effective contrast is apparent in a different way when, shortly afterwards, Aurelius cheerfully greets Dorigen in the street and asks her where she is going. In reply, she sobs out:

> 'Unto the gardyn, as myn housbonde bad,
> My trouthe for to holde, allas! allas! (1512–3)

Chaucer also makes his narrative more resonant by his use of vivid symbolic images. The garden is a good example: as in *The Merchant's Tale*, the garden is a place of significant happenings, as the Garden of Eden in the Bible was. It is in the medieval walled garden that lover's meetings take place, and that temptations arise. Here Aurelius declares his love to Dorigen, and she is on her way to the garden to find him when he meets her towards the end of the poem. The dance similarly represents more than the trivial occupation of idle courtiers: it can suggest actual love-making, and in Aurelius's dancing before Dorigen there is an element of masculine display. Dorigen longs to see her husband 'on the daunce go' (921) instead of Aurelius, whose wish-fulfillment vision conjured up by the clerk of Orleans involves both himself and Dorigen, dancing at the same time.

The most striking image in the poem is of course that of the rocks, which, though 'grisly' in appearance, actually safeguard the marriage of Dorigen and Arveragus. While they are in sight, Aurelius cannot lay claim to Dorigen. Their presence manifests God's loving providence rather than the reverse: the attempt to tamper with the natural objects that He has created leads to almost irremediable disaster, which is only avoided, at last, by the adherence to 'trouthe' – which takes its origin from God himself – of Arveragus, Dorigen and Aurelius, and the generosity (including the clerk's) which flows from it.

Rhetoric

Before beginning his tale, the Franklin says that his will be a 'bare and pleyne' (720) account, because he never learnt rhetoric and is ignorant of the 'colours' by means of which rhetoricians adorn their discourses. Of course the tale that he tells – being written by a great poet – is very far from being bare and plain: image and symbol, lively dialogue and carefully chosen patterns of repetition (for example, the reiteration of 'trouthe' which draws our attention to this important concept) make this tale a distinguished work of literary art. It is partly by means of rhetoric, in the best sense of the word, that the story makes its impact, for rhetoric was the art of effective persuasive speech and writing. We now associate the term with florid or vapid elaboration, and to some extent such an association was also made in Chaucer's time. Chaucer knew how to use this art with discrimination, but he could make fun of its clumsy use, as he does when the Franklin tells us that 'th'orisonte hath reft the sonne his lyght,/This is as muche to seye as it was nyght!' (1017–8). The Franklin's disclaimer at the beginning also makes us more aware of the context of the tale – the ongoing pilgrimage and the different story-tellers with their immense variety of tales and techniques. We feel that we are in the hands of a reliable, straightforward narrator when the Franklin begins, and when the tale ends, we are once more reminded of its teller when he turns to his audience, involving them still more closely with the question, 'Which was the mooste fre, as thynketh yow?' (1622). Such a question was in keeping with medieval literary convention, but the device still works for us today, inviting us to ponder on the story and the lasting values that give it substance.

The Physician's Tale

No linking passage connects this tale with any preceding one and it is not known for certain where Chaucer meant it to come. In some ways it resembles the stories in Chaucer's *The Legend of Good Women*, and may have been written before most of the other *Canterbury Tales*. Chaucer knew two earlier versions of the story of Virginia, one by the Roman historian Livy (59BC–AD17), the other from the French poem the *Roman de la Rose*.

The story

A knight has a young daughter, Virginia, his only child, who is not only very beautiful, but also very virtuous, and very dear to him. One day when accompanying her mother to the temple, she is seen by a wicked judge, Apius, who at once conceives a lustful desire for her. Knowing that she is well protected by her family, he devises a scheme to gain possession of her. He engages a churl to testify that Virginia is his runaway servant, and summons her father, Virginius, to answer the charge that he is harbouring her. The judge does not allow Virginius to make any defence, but insists that Virginia should be at once given up to him for 'restoration' to the churl. When Virginius sees that he can in no way avoid surrendering his daughter to the wicked judge, he calls her to him, tells her of the situation and explains that he has no choice but to kill her to preserve her from dishonour. She is deeply distressed, but freely submits to her father's decision. Later, when the facts of the case come to light, both the judge and his accomplice are appropriately punished.

COMMENTARY: Chaucer's version of this traditional story is movingly told, building up suspense and a sense of growing menace that can still engage the attention of the modern reader. Read at the purely literal level, it is of course an unlikely tale; though equally dreadful events are by no means unknown today. It makes more sense for us now, perhaps, if we read it as a story about the vulnerability, rarity and preciousness of the beautiful and the good, which are all too easily destroyed. It also contains the truth that we may destroy what we love most, accidentally, or from the best but mistaken motives. The story is an example of the kind of tale that Chaucer and his contemporaries found satisfying and believed to be true, because at the deepest symbolic level it *is* true.

The Physician's Tale begins with a typically medieval description of its heroine, in which we are told that in creating Virginia, Nature surpassed herself. Careful upbringing reinforced the good work, and the Doctor continues with an address to those reponsible for the care and education of young girls, and a reminder to parents to discipline their children as necessary. Though this passage does nothing to further the story, it is a good example of the worldly wisdom that the fourteenth-century audience appreciated, and such helpful advice is not inappropriate in the mouth of the experienced Doctor who gives it.

The Pardoner's Introduction, Prologue and Tale

The Physician's Tale seems particularly to appeal to the Host, whose emotional reaction to it is vigorously expressed, as is his approval of its teller. The effect upon the Host is such indeed, that he feels a need for an antidote to the strong feeling that it has provoked – 'a draughte of moyste and corny ale' (315), perhaps, or at least a more cheerful story. He calls upon the Pardoner to provide something more amusing, which he is very ready to do as soon as he has refreshed himself too. The

Pardoner's willingness to follow on provokes a minor outcry from the 'gentils', however: they say they want none of his ribaldry, but prefer 'some moral thyng' from which they can gain wisdom. The Pardoner promises to comply with their wishes when he has had his drink.

The Pardoner's Prologue

In his Prologue, the Pardoner explains his preaching technique: how he goes from one rural congregation to another, always preaching from the same text: 'The love of money is the root of all evil' (334, 426). By doing this, he enriches himself, for he is expert in persuading people to make donations.

COMMENTARY: In the *Roman de la Rose* a character called Fals Semblant preaches a sermon in which, like the Pardoner, he reveals the wicked ways in which he deceives his hearers to his own advantage. Chaucer certainly knew this passage, but he goes far beyond it in the Pardoner's Prologue. He creates a picture of the country congregations exploited by the greed of the Pardoner, making us aware of his victims, as well as of the techniques which he has perfected by years of practice.

The Pardoner explains how he produces his voice so as to be clearly heard, how he demonstrates his right to preach by displaying his credentials, and how he impresses his hearers by speaking a few words of Latin. Then he really gets going: first he displays what he claims is a relic, and appeals to the desire for gain as well as to the anxieties of his country congregation. The use of the bone from a holy Jew's sheep, he claims, will keep flocks and herds healthy, and cause them to increase. He then turns to another topic, addressing the women in the congregation: the wondrous bone also cures jealousy, preventing husbands from mistrusting their wives. After this, he turns to the men again and displays a mitten that brings about better harvests, and then addressing the whole congregation, he says anyone present who is guilty of 'synne horrible' (379), any woman who has cuckolded her husband, will be unable to come up and make their offerings. So he adds emotional blackmail and intimidation to the exploitation of his hearers' greed and natural anxieties, solely, (as he explains in 403 and 424) for his own enrichment. He knows his audience and he despises them, as his contemptuous comment on 'lewed peple' (437) makes clear; he does not care how poor they are, as long as he can exploit them and avoid poverty himself.

In describing how he preaches, the Pardoner creates a vivid picture of the credulous, slow-witted rural congregation and their world. He mentions the cows, calves, sheep and oxen, and their diseases; the crops of wheat and oats; the guilty wife and the enraged husband, the special soup that may be used to allay his jealousy. Chaucer, by his choice of concrete imagery, gives a sharp sense of the everyday work of the Pardoner too, as he makes his voice ring out like a bell, produces his bogus relics – rags and bones – stretching out his neck like a dove on a barn, his hands moving all the time as he gesticulates. In flow the pence, the groats, the gold and silver, the money and the gifts in kind of wool, cheese and wheat. But the Pardoner's persuasive dove-like cooing turns to something less agreeable if he fails to get what he wants: he can sting, and like a poisonous reptile he spits out venom under the guise of holiness.

The Pardoner knows and does not hesitate to admit that he is 'a ful vicious man' (459), indeed he seems entirely without shame and positively proud of his shameless wickedness. How are we as readers to respond to his confession? Do people give themselves away like this? It is of course true that they are sometimes proud and do boast of their evil deeds, especially when such deeds involve imposing upon and deceiving other people. It must also be remembered that the confession relates to a medieval convention which did not aim at total psychological realism, though the concrete detail with which Chaucer enriches the Pardoner's declaration gives it a vitality not found in earlier examples, such as the sermon of Fals Semblant.

The Pardoner's Tale

The tale, which is on the same theme as the Prologue, is set in Flanders, where a group of young people encourage each other in living a sinful life. The Pardoner then condemns the gluttony, drunkenness, gambling and swearing in which such people indulge, before beginning his account of the three revellers in the tavern who set out to kill Death. These three young men are drinking in an inn when they hear a funeral procession, ask the boy who has died, and when they hear that it is a friend of theirs, carried off by Death, decide to search for Death and slay him. Swearing loyalty to each other with dreadful oaths, they set off, and meet an old man. They speak to him rudely and ask him where Death is. He points out a tree in the far distance, under which they will find Death, he says. Off they go, and find a great pile of gold coins there, so they draw lots to decide who is to go to fetch food and drink from the town, while the others remain behind to guard the treasure until night. The young man who goes for food, buys poison and puts it in the wine; the other two plan to murder their friend when he returns, and to share the gold. When he gets back, they kill him, refresh themselves with the wine, and die immediately.

The Pardoner then denounces homicide and other sins, and urges his hearers to make offerings and receive pardon from him, reminding them of their good fortune in having him with them. He suggests that the Host shall seek pardon first; but the infuriated Host rudely says what he thinks should be done to the Pardoner for suggesting such a thing. They both become so angry that the Knight has to intervene to reconcile them, making them kiss each other before they all ride on.

COMMENTARY: *The Pardoner's Tale* is an *exemplum*, an exemplary tale by means of which a medieval preacher could illustrate a particular point in a memorable way. The tale of the three young men who seek to slay Death is a very ancient one, thought to be ultimately of Eastern origin. Chaucer's version places it in a contemporary setting, enriches it with symbolic imagery and gives it dramatic power by means of skilfully handled dialogue and narration.

In the first part of the tale, the Pardoner builds up atmosphere by speaking of the wicked ways of the young people in Flanders: the denunciation of sin of course makes for some colourful description. The Pardoner varies his approach by making learned references (to Lot and Herod (485 and 489) in the Bible; and to Seneca, the Roman writer (492)) and rhetorical exclamations (such as 'O glotonye, ful of cursednesse!' (498) and 'O wombe! O bely! O stynkyng cod' (534)), as well as by his vivid description of the cooks at work (538–43), and a dramatic imitation of a drunken man snoring (551–4). He shows his own worldly knowledge of London and even of different wines when he refers to Fish Street and Cheapside, where Spanish and French wines are sold (562–71), just as later on he quotes the blasphemous oaths and technical terms used by gamblers (651–5), suggesting that he is acquainted at first hand with the underworld of vice.

The theme of the pledged word, which underlines *The Franklin's Tale*, is taken up (though more indirectly) again here, in the emphasis on oaths and on words; and the gamblers' oaths, such as 'By Goddes precious herte', and 'By his nayles' (651), introduce a vein of religious imagery which plays an important part in the total effect of the poem.

The prelude on the various sins builds up atmosphere for the tale of the three revellers and also helps to transport the reader away from the everyday world, through the disreputable scenes in Flanders, to the inmost world of the story in which different planes of reality are combined, with a haunting, almost surrealistic effect. Death, for example, is introduced on two planes at once, as a natural event which has carried off the friend of the three revellers, and as a personified figure 'a privee theef' (675) who has come, armed with a spear and ready to attack; then there is a further shift to the plane of spiritual values, 'Beth redy for to meete hym evermoore' (683). The revellers are eager to meet him, but not in the spiritual sense; and one of them ends up by declaring 'He shal be slayn . . . er it be nyght!' (700–1). They have forgotten, it seems, that only Christ can vanquish death; their proud undertaking to do what Christ alone could do is sacrilegious. Now they swear oaths 'To lyve and dyen ech of hem for oother,/ As though he were his owene ybore brother' (703-4), grisly oaths, on different parts of Christ's body. But in reality, oaths mean nothing to them, as is later seen.

The story is made more haunting and impressive by its characters. They have a symbolic resonance, representing three stages of life: first there is the boy, who informs them about the funeral, and perhaps represents the uncorrupted innocence of youth, as he quotes his mother's spiritual teaching (683-4). Then there are the three revellers, who are not distinguished from each other – they do not need to be, for they are equal in wickedness and recklessness – and who are in the prime of life. The old man whom they meet half a mile from the tavern is a mysterious figure. He longs to die but cannot; the wisdom of age shows him where and how the young men will meet death, but not where and when he will die himself as he restlessly walks on and on knocking on the ground, his 'mother's gate', and saying 'Leeve mooder, leet me in' (731). The gratuitous and brutal insolence with which the revellers address this old man suggests the 'pride of life' which drives them on to their untimely death, ironically causing them to die when the old man cannot.

The revellers insist that the old man should direct them to where they can meet Death, and again in a different way, their oaths take on a blasphemous tone. As before they had sworn that they would die for each other (703) (as Christ did for mankind), so now they invoke St John and the holy sacrament (752 and 757) to make the old man comply with their wishes. Their angry, menacing demand is ironically reinforced by oaths which invoke the disciple whom Jesus is said to have particularly loved, and the sacrament in which His love is manifested to mankind. The reference to the holy sacrament is taken up again still more ironically at a later stage in the story.

The old man answers courteously, pointing out the grove – the very tree (actually an oak) where Death is to be found. Our imaginative gaze follows his directions, focussing in on the precise spot. The revellers run to it and instantly find – not Death, it seems – but treasure, so they abandon their former quest, and plan to wait until night falls to carry off the gold. The treasure, however, turns out to be not life-enhancing, but death-bringing. To keep them going, the youngest is to fetch bread and wine from the town, food which reminds us of the 'hooly sacrement' mentioned earlier (757). The bread and wine of the sacrament of the Last Supper represents the body and blood of Christ, whose death on the cross brings eternal life to the believing Christian. But the bread and wine fetched by the youngest reveller brings not life but death to his fellows – spiritual as well as bodily death because they die guilty of the sin of homicide. Chaucer could have made the young man fetch ale and meat, or simply food, but the choice of this food has particularly ironic undertones. The food which symbolises the supreme sacrifice of love for others is poisoned, and supplied from hatred and greed and selfishness. The poison sold by the apothecary is intended to destroy vermin, and so it does, but ironically its victims are human vermin.

The story gathers momentum as it draws to its swift dénouement. The glimpse of the normal everyday world of the town with its apothecary's shop, its commonplace problems, the ravages of rats, polecats and other vermin on poultry yards, makes more horrible the deliberate wickedness with which the youngest reveller plans to poison his two friends and hurries off to the next street to borrow bottles for the wine. Skilfully the Pardoner ends the story without further ado: as the two older revellers kill their fellow, and then sit down to make merry with the drink that he had brought, they choose the wrong bottle and die.

Though the story ends here, the tale does not. We return to the scene of the pilgrimage once more, and see that the Pardoner wishes to lose no opportunity of turning his expertise to his own advantage, as he forthwith invites the pilgrims to make their contributions. But ironically, instead of prompting them to buy pardons, he only succeeds in driving the Host into a frenzy of anger; and the insults offered him in turn render the Pardoner speechless with rage. It is such anger that leads to homicide, and the Knight has to intervene. In the last section of the tale, Chaucer shows how difficult – and how necessary – it is for human beings to love one another, as he explores yet another aspect of human nature and relationships.

To sum up, this tale – one of Chaucer's most memorable and powerful – depends for its success first upon its great variety of effects, as the Pardoner demonstrates his preaching techniques. Through the excellence of the dialogue, its characters are brought to life and differentiated. Its symbolic imagery and its ironies are complemented by glimpses of normality, by means of which the story moves on two planes at once. Its events take place simultaneously in the everyday world of tavern and town, as well as on the spiritual plane where men may travel, by their own deliberate choice, inexorably towards damnation, along the 'croked wey' (761) that is both literally a path and a process. Finally, the figure of the Pardoner enhances the effect of the tale, as he puts all his energy into preaching against the very sin of which he is pre-eminently guilty, without realising that he is condemned out of his own mouth, and has completely given his own game away.

The Shipman's Tale

The tale belongs to another group, and appears to have originally been intended for the Wife of Bath, for lines 11 to 14 are clearly intended to be spoken by a woman. It has, indeed, no special appropriateness to its teller. It is another example of *fabliau*, and is one of Chaucer's most amusing and beautifully told tales.

The story

A merchant at St Denis has a lively, beautiful wife, and a great friend who is a monk, who is always welcome at his house. On one occasion when the monk comes to stay, the merchant is particularly busy and so rises early. So also does the monk, who goes into the garden where the wife comes to him in great consternation. The monk comments on her pale face, so she tells him how unkind her husband is to her. She owes a hundred francs and dares not tell her husband. The monk agrees to help her, saying that he will bring her the money soon, and kisses her warmly. So she happily goes away. Soon after this the husband has to leave on a business trip, but before he goes, the monk privately asks for the loan of a hundred francs for a deal he needs to make; this the merchant readily gives to him. The next Sunday, while the merchant is still away, the monk comes to his house with the money, in exchange for which the wife has agreed to spend the night with him, and a merry time they have. When next the merchant and the monk meet, the monk says that he has repaid his loan to the wife in the merchant's absence. The merchant goes home, makes love to his wife to their mutual satisfaction, and then reproaches her for not having told him that the money had been repaid. She instantly replies that she assumed the money was given to her as a present, and that she has spent it all on clothes, so as to do her husband credit. She says she will pay him back in bed, and seeing that there was nothing else to be done, he forgives her.

COMMENTARY: This high spirited story of how a husband is unknowingly outwitted and cuckolded by an ingenious monk is based on a typical *fabliau* situation, but unlike many such tales, it ends with all the characters happy and satisfied. And they are all pleasant characters. The merchant is not only highly successful and prosperous, but his personality is warm, generous and friendly and he appears also to be – as an ideal husband should – 'fressh abedde' (177). Unlike most *fabliau* husbands, he is neither old nor jealous. The wife is cheerful, affectionate and sprightly. Don John, the monk, is liked and indeed respected by everyone, and though he contrives an act of treachery against his friend the merchant, since the latter does not know about it, no-one is really any the worse off. The tale is pervaded by an atmosphere of uninhibited enjoyment – of the good things of life in general, including sex and friendship. A cheerful, ungrudging spirit prompts the actions of each of the characters, and even the activities of the agreeable Don John do not significantly deprive the merchant of anything, and may be said even to contribute to domestic harmony.

The tale is told with a good deal of surface realism. The competent monk's supervision of the granaries and barns of his monastery, the merchant's business trips and grave explanation to his wife of the hard work needed to succeed in business (224–38), as well as her supervision of the household, recreate some aspects of the medieval world of work. Even more striking is the psychological realism of the passage in which Don John comments on the wife's paleness, enquiring whether her husband is keeping her from sleep and blushing meanwhile at his lustful thoughts. Such realism gives substance to a tale which depends for its effect mainly upon a very ingenious plot: our enjoyment is increased because Chaucer enables us to visualise the situation so well. The lively dialogue also adds to the realism, differentiating the characters and expressing their moods, in dramatic little scenes such as Don John's meeting with the wife in the garden. Her subsequent dialogue with her husband is full of exclamations and questions; and its exuberant nature reveals her delight in Don John's previous declaration of love and offer of help, not to mention his enthusiastic embrace and kisses. There is serious business talk, good friendly advice on the subject of health before Don John asks for the loan, and a homely dialogue between husband and wife in bed which suggests a happy marriage relationship (despite the wife's quick-witted but shameless lie – as usual in *fabliau* the woman gets away with her tricks).

The narration is also distinguished by its unity of tone and tight structure. There are no learned digressions, no disjunctions, but the story flows on until it satisfactorily resolves itself at the end. Chaucer does not include, as in *The Miller's Tale*, parodic elements or satire, and there is little irony, except in the trick played upon the husband. The narration is not only economical, but also has effective touches of humour – for example, the half-rhetorical question:

Who was so welcome as my lord daun John,
Oure deere cosyn, ful of curteisye? (68–9)

This is immediately followed by lines which suggest, in concrete terms, good reasons for his being welcome: he brings with him two jugs of wine. In *The Shipman's Tale* there are no hidden depths of meaning, but it succeeds entirely as an entertainment.

The Prioress's Prologue and Tale

The Host congratulates the Shipman on his tale and comments on the cunning tricks of monks, before turning to the Prioress, whom he very respectfully invites to tell the next tale. She willingly agrees to do so, and after a pious invocation to the Blessed Virgin Mary, tells a story very different in every way from that of the Shipman's.

The story

In an otherwise Christian city in Asia there is a Jewish quarter, and at one end of this district there is a school for the Christian children. This story is about a small boy of seven whose mother is a widow. One day he hears the older boys at his school singing a hymn in honour of the Blessed Virgin Mary. As it is in Latin he does not understand the words, but he longs to learn it, and so an older friend teaches him words and music. He sings it every day on his way home from school, for although he is so young, he has a special love for the Blessed Virgin Mary. Unfortunately, however, Satan stirs up hatred in the hearts of the Jews, and they kill the child and throw his body into a ditch. His mother, in great distress when he does not come home, searches everywhere for him, until at last by a miracle, she hears his song ring out and finds his body. The Christians then carry it, still singing, to the church and the abbot asks the child how it is that he can still sing. He explains the miracle which has enabled him to do so, and says that he will continue to sing until a grain placed on his tongue by the Blessed Virgin Mary is removed. The abbot then takes away the grain so that he can find rest, and praising the Virgin Mary, the Christians bury his little body in a marble tomb.

COMMENTARY: For the *Prologue to The Prioress's Tale* and the tale itself Chaucer used a stanzaic form, rhyme royal. The Prologue is a formal but lyrical invocation to the Virgin Mary, the 'white lylye flour' (461), and source of goodness and spiritual health. The Prioress addresses the Virgin Mary as 'mooder Mayde! O mayde Mooder', and as a 'bussh unbrent' (467–8): Mary is paradoxically and miraculously both a virgin and a mother, and traditionally compared to the burning bush from which Moses heard God speak to him, because her body held Christ, as the bush held God. Devotion to the Virgin Mary was widespread in the fourteenth century, as many representations in art (such as the Wilton diptych in the National Gallery, London) suggest, and such devotion was certainly felt by Chaucer, one of whose very earliest poems was in praise of Mary.

Legends of the miracles of the Virgin Mary were very popular in the Middle Ages, and there were many versions of this particular tale, which Chaucer so appropriately assigns to the devout and tender-hearted Prioress. Its inclusion extends the range of the different types of story that make up *The Canterbury Tales* and adds to our knowledge and understanding of medieval people, for it shows up both their capacity for sympathy, sensitivity and deep emotion, and its counterpart in intolerance. To the modern reader, the anti-semitism in the tale is deeply shocking, particularly when the murderers of the child are punished, and it seems ironic that such deeds should be related by the Prioress.

We should perhaps remind ourselves of the frequency with which fanaticism at the present day leads to equally barbarous reprisals – we have not yet succeeded in making humanity and tolerance universally prevalent. The Prioress, in expressing her antipathy to Jews, is of course, expressing current medieval attitudes: the Jews (of whom there were few in England at the time, so she was not likely ever to have met any) were abhorred on the grounds that they had crucified Christ; and popular prejudice soon generated other reasons for hating them too, as sectarian quarrels still generate hatred in the twentieth century. The terrible punishments with which the murderers and their accomplices are visited in *The Prioress's Tale* also have to be seen in the light of what was accepted as the norm in the Middle Ages, a time when savage penalties were usual (see, for example, the fate which befalls the carter and inn-keeper, both guilty of murder, as related in *The Nun's Priest's Tale* (3058–62)). Belief in spiritual reality put bodily suffering in a different perspective; for example, the soul's health often came before physical well-being. Chaucer also makes this point explicitly in *The Second Nun's Tale*, in which St Cecilia says:

Men myghten dreden wel and skilfully
This lyf to lese, myn owene deere brother,
If this were lyvynge oonly and noon oother.

But there is bettre lif in oother place,
That nevere shal be lost, ne drede thee noght (320–4)

If the vengeance upon the Jews strikes us as crude, the more tender feelings with which the tale is concerned are very highly developed. The two little boys going home from school together, the one teaching his friend the song as they go along, and the desperation of the mother, searching everywhere for her child when he does not return, are movingly presented scenes. The religious feeling that pervades the poem is probably less accessible to most readers now, but it no less contributes to the prevailing atmosphere of tender affection, expressed in terms of friendship, motherly love and religious devotion. The child's cruel death followed by the throwing of his body into the latrine is contrasted to the image of heavenly bliss represented by allusions to *The Revelation of St John the Divine* in the Bible, an account of a vision of Christ as the Lamb of God, accompanied by a great host of martyrs. The little boy's horrible death admits him to eternal life, where the innocent 'synge a songe al newe' (584). Heaven and earth are contrasted again as the vision of the Lamb gives place to the frantic grief of the mother, but one of the meanings that the poem communicates is that we must realise that heaven and earth converge. The mother's search continues until she approaches the place where her child's body has been thrown, and at this point again the loathesome image of the pit is succeeded by images of the permanent joy of heaven: the child is now a 'gemme of chastite' (609), an emerald, the ruby of martyrdom. The imperishable beauty of precious stones of which St John speaks in *The Revelation* suggests, in a surrealistic symbolical way, the true state of the murdered child, for he has become a part of the unchanging splendour and glory of heaven, and is alive on the plane of spiritual reality. (For a similar conception, a poem known as *Pearl*, by a contemporary of Chaucer's, also makes use of jewel-imagery from the same biblical source. The poet sees a vision of his dead child as a pearl-maiden in the New Jerusalem, of which St John speaks in *The Revelation*).

Like *The Shipman's Tale* before it, this story is superbly told in its own very different way. Pathos and piety pervade it, but despite its brevity, it achieves a considerable variety of effects. The contrasting images of earthly horror and celestial beauty have been mentioned, and these give a richness of texture to the tale, as do the touches of dialogue. There are elements of drama and suspense, for example when the mother searches for her child. Chaucer gives us a sense of the narrator's presence (in such phrases as 'As I have seyd', 'I seye' and in such exclamations as 'O martir', 'O grete God', 'O yonge Hugh of Lyncoln') lending a greater immediacy to the tale. But it must be remembered that it should be interpreted as the tale assigned to the Prioress, and not as a dramatic monologue intended to be consistently revelatory of her attitudes and character.

The Prologue and Tale of Sir Thopas

The Prioress's Tale was very well received by its hearers, who seem to have been awed into silence by it, until the Host begins to make jokes and calls on Chaucer to tell 'a tale of myrthe'. He agrees, offering 'a rhyme that he learned long ago' and begins.

Sir Thopas

Chaucer's tale is regarded as such a failure by the Host that he interrupts him and tells him to stop. In it, Chaucer satirises the old fashioned tail-rhyme chivalric romances that were very popular in his time, but unfortunately the Host lacks the literary sophistication to appreciate the subtlety of *Sir Thopas*. Without some knowledge of these old romances it is difficult for the modern reader, too, to realise to the full how funny *Sir Thopas* is; but nevertheless it is easy to see that Sir Thopas is a very odd sort of knight to be the hero of a romance. The shining armour that a knight might be expected to wear has given place to leather shoes, brown hose and robe; and Sir Thopas's complexion (white as bread with rose-red lips and a yellow beard) almost suggests a medieval heroine rather than a doughty warrior. Despite his unmanly appearance, Sir Thopas considers that no ordinary lady is worthy to be his love – though many are smitten with love for him – for he is determined to have only an elf-queen as his mate. Chaucer thus makes him ridiculous, while he also parodies the magical elements common in such romances, as he does again later on when Thopas encounters a giant called Sir Olifaunt. Thopas rapidly draws back when the giant begins to throw stones at him, after saying that he will come back next day to fight, when he is fully equipped. When Sir Thopas gets home, he announces that the giant that he intends to fight has three heads: though he seemed to have only one before. Then, before putting on his armour, Sir Thopas consumes some sweet wine, gingerbread and other unmanly items of food. In this part of the poem, Chaucer satirises the hackneyed descriptions of feasts with which medieval storytellers sometimes filled out their tales, as well as a similar set-piece in medieval romance, the arming of the hero. We have a very detailed account of the underwear and other garments that Thopas puts on, but the armour itself is made of all the wrong materials; and he finally mounts a dapple-grey steed that sounds more appropriate for a middle-aged medieval lady, as it gently ambles off with its strange rider.

There the 'First Fit' of the tale ends, but Chaucer immediately starts on a second, asking his audience of 'knight and lady free' to 'hold their mouths' (891–2) while he tells them of battle, chivalry and ladies' love-tokens, and of how Sir Thopas goes on his way. But before he has finished his fifth stanza, and before his hero has had time to do anything, the Host interrupts indignantly and Chaucer has to stop. Perhaps it was just as well – any more would have been tedious, since one of the points made by *Sir Thopas* is that in such tales which seem to go on and on for ever nothing of real interest ever happens.

In *Sir Thopas*, Chaucer also parodies the jog-trot meter of the tail-rhyme romances, and their clumsy, forced rhymes. Minstrels tended to pad out lines and stanzas with rather empty meaningless filler-phrases, such as 'in good intent' and 'as I yow telle may', and with doublets like 'chaast and no lechour', 'By dale and eek by downe', 'ride or goon'. All the tired old clichés of such stories are piled on to the very slender narrative framework of the tale of *Sir Thopas* until it collapses in the face of the Host's impatience; but before this happens, Chaucer has made his point in a very amusing way.

The Prologue and Tale of Melibee

The Host's rudely-worded complaint about Chaucer's rubbishy rhymes is followed by an invitation to try again in another medium, and so he offers 'a litel thyng in prose'. To most modern readers *The Tale of*

Melibee is a very indigestible work, but it was a treatise which was highly valued in the Middle Ages. Its Latin original was translated into French, from which Chaucer's is a close translation. The serious discussion of various ethical problems which it provides was appreciated by Chaucer's contemporaries because the issues were seen to be important and the opportunities of hearing them intelligently discussed were few. This allegorical work has a slender narrative thread: the rich and powerful Melibeus is distressed because his daughter Sophie has been assaulted and severely injured, and he ponders on how to react. His first impulse is to take his revenge, but his wife Prudence argues him out of the idea. She urges him to be patient, and at the end his enemies repent and he forgives them, in the hope that 'God of his endeless mercy wole at the tyme of our diyinge forgeven us oure giltes that we han trespassed to hym in this wrecched world . . . and bryngen us to the blisse that nevere hath ende' (1882–87). *The Tale of Melibee* contains much traditional wisdom in a form which Chaucer's contemporaries found memorable. It can still remind us of the brave struggle of the men of the Middle Ages to make humane and enlightened attitudes prevail over the evil impulses and violent human passions which, centuries later, we are still unable to control.

The Monk's Prologue and Tale

When Chaucer's tale ends, the Host says how much he wishes his wife was like Melibee's wife Prudence, and gives a brief indication of some of his marital problems. Then he turns to the Monk, commenting rather freely on his fine physique, and lamenting tht such virile members of the population are vowed to celibacy. The Monk listens patiently to these remarks, and then offers to tell the pilgrims some of the tragedies he knows. He says that he has a hundred such stories, carefully explaining what the term 'tragedy' implies.

The Monk's definition of tragedy enables us to see exactly what the medieval conception of the genre was: the story, as recorded in old books, of a man who, from great prosperity and a high position, falls into a state of misery, in which he dies. The idea of the 'fatal flaw' which brings about a man's downfall, as we see in Shakespeare's tragedies, does not apply. The popular image of Fortune and her wheel, on which men are carried up to a position of honour, power and success, and then inexorably overcome by misfortune and dashed down to death, represents in pictorial form this medieval concept.

Chaucer modelled *The Monk's Tale* on a Latin work by Boccaccio. The Monk's tragedies – he relates only seventeen, before the Knight begs him to stop – are varied in length, some consisting of a single stanza. He begins with Lucifer, the rebel angel, whose fall was presumably the most spectacular, then proceeds to Adam and Sampson. Hercules is next, and thereafter the Monk mingles biblical and classical 'heroes'. He includes a queen, Cenobia, and then moves to tragedies of more recent times, such as the terrible story of Count Ugolino of Pisa in Dante's *Inferno*, starved to death in a tower with his children. Nero (Roman Emperor from AD54–68) who was thought by some ancient authors to have ordered the burning of Rome in AD64, and Julius Caesar (102–44BC), the Roman general, dictator and prose writer, also appear in the series, which ends with Croesus (*d*. 546), the last king of Lydia, and a man of immense wealth, who, in this version, is hanged.

Such stories afforded Chaucer little scope for his genius (though his contemporaries enjoyed them), so after a while he allows the Knight to interrupt the Monk and call for something more cheerful.

The Nun's Priest's Prologue and Tale

After the Knight has asked for a more entertaining story from the Monk, the Host joins in, asking him to talk about hunting, but he refuses. The Host then turns to the Nun's Priest and in his usual coarse, hearty manner invites him to tell something cheering, which the Nun's Priest undertakes to do.

The story

A poor old widow, who lives in a little cottage, has a fine cock, Chauntecleer, and seven hens, of which his favourite is called Pertelote. One night Chauntecleer has a bad dream of a tawny beast menacing him, and he tells the dream to Pertelote. She reproves him for being afraid, insists that his bad dream was caused by a disordered stomach, and tells him to take some laxatives. Chauntecleer replies that the dream should be regarded as a warning against some impending disaster, and lists several cases of warning dreams that had come true. After quoting a number of learned works on the subject, he goes out into the farmyard, clucking and crowing cheerfully. But unhappily a fox is lurking in the yard. Chauntecleer sees him and is on the point of fleeing, when the fox begins to flatter him. Chauntecleer, forgetting all about his dream, soon succumbs and begins to crow to prove his powers. At once the fox seizes him and carries him off. A tremendous hue and cry ensues, as all the farmyard gives chase, until Chauntecleer thinks of a ruse to make the fox open his mouth. It succeeds and he escapes to a tree, proof against further persuasion by the fox. He has learnt his lesson.

COMMENTARY: The well-known folk-tale or fable of the cock and the fox has never been more delightfully told than in Chaucer's version. The realism with which the poor widow's humble household is described suddenly explodes into fantasy as Chauntecleer is introduced. He is made to sound important and dignified: his voice is compared to an organ and his crowing more accurately timed than an abbey clock. The brilliance of his comb, his bill, his feet and claws, and his plumage are described in terms of heraldic colours, and the references to the castle wall and the lily-flower place the cock in a chivalric context. We are suddenly in a world of heraldic splendour in which the hens have become courtly ladies. Chauntecleer loves the 'faire damoysele Pertelote' (2870) with courtly devotion, and together they sing a medieval love lyric 'My lief is faren in londe!' (2879), the words of which have survived to this day.

Chaucer shifts the focus of the poem back and forth between the animal and the human. This is a common feature of fables, in which animals behave like human beings, to remind us of how often we tend to behave like animals. With Chauntecleer and Pertelote, the alternation of animal and human characteristics is a source of brilliant comedy, because of the precision with which their human aspects are defined. No sooner has Pertelote been introduced as a courtly lady than we are told how well she has conducted herself since she was a week-old chick. Her well considered prescription for Chauntecleer's disorder, in which she recommends accepted fourteenth-century herbal remedies for human beings, concludes with the injunction to 'Pekke hem up right' (2967), and husband and wife are at once diminished again to farmyard fowls. Most delightfully, after Chauntecleer's impressive display of learning, comes his loving compliment to Pertelote, 'Ye been so scarlet reed aboute youre yen' (3161); followed by a swift return to the human level when he quotes a Latin saying against women, and then purposely mistranslates it (for her benefit) in a complimentary sense, knowing that she does not understand the language. We hardly know – such is the speed with which Chaucer switches the focus – whether we are in the farmyard or in the court of Richard II, when Chaucer says:

This Chauntecleer his wynges gan to bete
As man that koude his traysoun nat espie,
So was he ravysshed with his flaterie. (3322–4)

Beneath the surface of this entertaining story, however, lies a serious consideration of the significance of dreams, in which Chaucer was deeply interested. Do they, as Pertelote asserts, arise simply from physical causes, or can they be reliably interpreted as warnings or revelations from God? A Latin text, Cicero's *Somnium Scipionis*, with the commentary on it by Macrobius (see page 38) was a source of much medieval dream-theory. It was believed that there were several different categories of dream, ranging from direct communications from some spiritual power, to the dreams arising from one's waking preoccupations or bodily disorders. Some people were sceptical, like Pertelote, about the significance of dreams, and unwilling to accept that they had any value as revelations or warnings. Chauntecleer, of course, takes the opposite view, citing instances of dreams that had come true. Chaucer creates superb comedy out of Pertelote's scorn and her husband's credulity, and out of her fussy, though well-informed suggestions on medicine and diet; as also from Chauntecleer's ability to quote Cato, Macrobius, saints' lives, the Old Testament and so forth. The comedy is enhanced by the fact that so soon after insisting on the significance of dreams, he completely forgets all about the warning he had received and succumbs to the flattery of Russell the fox.

The story 'proves' that dreams are to be taken seriously, as foreshadowing future events. Pertelote is wrong about dreams and Chauntecleer was right to be alarmed – misogyny is another serious topic with which the tale deals. 'Wommennes conseils been ful ofte colde' (3256), we are told; and though Chauntecleer is shown to some extent as a hen-pecked husband, when Pertelote pours scorn on his fears and despises him for being a coward, he asserts his superiority by quoting and mistranslating for fun the Latin saying she cannot understand. The Nun's Priest disclaims any intention of slighting women. 'Thise been thé cokkes wordes, and nat myne' (3265), he says, but the point has been made. Since Adam fell as a result of Eve's misjudgment, women's advice is not to be trusted, and the dangers of following it are demonstrated again in this story.

But was Chauntecleer *predestined* to be caught by the fox, or was he free to avoid the danger of which his dream had warned him? Chaucer brings in another controversial topic, for in the fourteenth century there was much argument by learned men, such as 'Bisshop Bradwardyn' (3242), about free-will and predestination. It was one that seems to have interested him deeply. In *The Consolation of Philosophy* by Boethius (here referred to as 'Boece' (3242)), which Chaucer himself translated, there is a long discussion of how our free-will can be compatible with God's foreknowledge of what we are going to do. Chaucer also included a more serious passage of debate on the subject in *Troilus and Criseyde*, also drawn from Boethius. Here, though he refers to the seriousness of the 'greet disputisoun' (3238) which has involved so many learned men, he shows the Nun's Priest as unwilling to commit himself to either side in the argument: 'I wol nat han to do of swich mateere' (3251), he says. Nevertheless, destiny may not be avoided (3338), whether what happens to us is predestined or comes about in consequence of our own choices and actions. At the end of *The Knight's Tale*, Duke Theseus suggests that whatever befalls us, our destiny is worked out within the larger plan of the 'wise providence' that orders all things in the universe, implying that it is ultimately for our good.

Yet another topical matter which plays a part in the tale is the subject of court flattery, delicately handled as such a subject clearly needed to be when Chaucer was writing. He warns that many a false flatterer lurks within courts, as the fox lay in wait for the gullible Chauntecleer (3325–30). There is an allusion, too, to another contemporary matter, the Peasants' Revolt of 1381, and Jack Straw's rebellion. Such comments are rare in Chaucer's writing: he seldom chose to make even a passing comment on public events or the more unpleasant aspects of the age he lived in, taking as he did a larger view of human life than many writers do today.

Medical theories also feature in *The Nun's Priest's Tale*. Pertelote's remedies for a disordered stomach have been already mentioned, all of them – even the prescribed worms, which had been recommended for tertian fever by the Greek physician Dioscorides (first century AD) – medicines for human ailments in the Middle Ages. They indicate Chaucer's interest in and knowledge of this branch of learning, too, as do the references to Chauntecleer's temperament, and his natural desire to get away from the fox because 'a beest desireth flee fro his contrarie' (3279–80). It was generally believed that every object or creature had its contrary which it wished to avoid. *The Nun's Priest's Tale* is thus based in the best scientific knowledge of the time, though Chaucer's lightness of touch turns all to comedy.

Literary conventions and techniques as well as scientific theory and medical practice are drawn in to enrich the total effect. The poem as a whole is (like *The Rape of the Lock* by Alexander Pope (1688–1744)) a splendid example of the mock-heroic, in which trivial events are treated very seriously, as if they were on a level with major disasters. This is made especially clear when, for example, Chauntecleer is carried off, amid even greater outcry than there was at the fall of Troy, described by Homer in the *Iliad* and Virgil in the *Aeneid*. Chaucer next compares the uproar to that which occurred at the fall of Carthage, and when the Emperor Nero set Rome on fire; but the sounds of lamentation come, not from senator's wives, but from hens, accompanied by the barking of dogs and quacking of ducks as well as the shouts and yells of the farm workers. In order to make it all the more absurd Chaucer uses conventional rhetorical devices in an exaggerated way, for example when he exclaims 'O destinee ... O Venus ... O Gaufred ... O woful hennes' (3338–69). They add a mock solemnity to the episode in which the sin of pride brings about the downfall of our hero.

The story ends with some timelessly valid conclusions, as each party learns his lesson 'He who is blind when he ought to see does not deserve to succeed' says Chauntecleer (3430–1); and Russell the fox caps the comment with his own:

'Naye,' quod the fox, 'but God yere him meschaunce,
That is so indiscreet of governaunce
That jangleth whan he sholde holde his pees.' (3433–5)

So they have the last word in this brilliantly witty and amusing story of
human blindness, in which Chaucer's learning makes a sophisticated
and many-faceted comedy of the old folk-tale. The poem is longer than
the tale itself, however, and in the final lines the Nun's Priest adds his
own comment, seriously reminding his audience of St Paul's teaching
(*Romans*, 15:4) that all that is written, is written for our learning, and
advising them to take the serious message from the tale and forget the
rest. We are reminded of the solemn purpose of the pilgrimage and the
continuing journey of the participants, both through the English
countryside and through life itself.

The Second Nun's Prologue and Tale

Chaucer probably wrote the tale he assigns to the Second Nun rather
earlier in his career, probably after his first visit to Italy in 1372. It is a
fairly close translation from a Latin version and so lacks the originality
of such tales as the immediately preceding Nun's Priest's. Chaucer
obviously regarded it as a tale conducive to spiritual health: from it, its
hearers could take the 'morality' and the 'fruit', as the Nun's Priest urges
them to do from his own much more entertaining story. Chaucer must
have wanted to include it with the other tales as a story well worth
remembering, and the Second Nun was – like the Prioress with her
somewhat similar tale – just the person to tell it.

A Prologue comes first, in praise of the Virgin Mary (as with *The
Prioress's Tale*), to whom Chaucer had a special devotion throughout
his life. But first, four stanzas denounce idleness (a fault of which
Chaucer can never have been guilty), but which Chaucer's contemporary
Langland also bitterly condemned on the same grounds: that the idle
'devouren al that othere swynke' (eat up all that other people produce by
their hard work) (21). There follows an invocation to the Virgin Mary,
flower of all virgins, whose worship had much increased as a result of the
devotional writing of St Bernard (mentioned in line 30). As in the
Prologue to The Prioress's Tale, the Blessed Virgin Mary is addressed in
metaphorical images which indicate the special qualities that had been
attributed to her by earlier scholars. She is the 'welle of mercy' (37), a
'havene of refut [refuge]' (75). Such symbolic images had a strong
appeal for Chaucer's contemporaries. Even more strangely, and
paradoxically, Mary is referred to as the 'daughter of her Son', Jesus
(36). People prayed to her to be their advocate, asking her to beg Jesus to
have mercy on them, on the Day of Judgment.

The legend of St Cecilia which follows is an example of the kind of saint's life which Chaucer's contemporaries both liked and valued. It is full of human interest and feeling, as well as of the marvellous, indeed the miraculous. Cecilia is married to Valerian, but wishing in her piety to remain a virgin dedicated to God, she persuades her husband not to consummate the marriage, and converts him to her faith. When he goes home after being baptised by Pope Urban and finds Cecilia with an angel, he is so firmly convinced of the truth that he has just embraced that he converts his brother. When they are required by the wicked Almachius to worship idols, the two young men are martyred. Almachius claims that he has 'bothe power and auctoritee/To maken folk to dyen or to lyven' (471–2), but Cecilia points out to him that he only has the power to be a 'Ministre of deeth' (485), not to give life. At last, Cecilia too is martyred, but the memory of her exemplary life and death remains as an inspiration.

The Second Nun's Tale is very even in tone, a study in black and white compared with the colour and rich texture of *The Nun's Priest's Tale*. Its chief interest for us now is as a good example of a kind of story which had a very great appeal in the fourteenth century, but it is short enough to keep the modern reader's attention.

The Canon's Yeoman's Prologue and Tale

The Canon's Yeoman's Prologue

The pilgrimage is by this time well under way, for the pilgrims have reached the village of Boughton, when they are overtaken by a canon and the yeoman who attends him as his servant. In those days, a canon was a cleric attached to a religious order, living under the general rule of the order as a member of a self-governing community. Canons were not enclosed within the community, as monks were, but could lead more independent lives, rather like the canons who are attached to cathedrals in England at the present day.

Chaucer, reporting on the sudden arrival of two more pilgrims, mentions several times how the horses were sweating, and how fast they must have come – the Canon must have spurred his horse as if he was mad (576). It turns out that the Canon specialises in alchemy, a study about which Chaucer obviously knew a good deal, and we soon begin to guess that the haste with which the two horsemen have ridden up and attached themselves to the pilgrims may have more to do with eluding pursuers than with any pious intentions. Their dramatic arrival on the scene at the conclusion of the serious, devotional legend of St Cecilia makes a striking contrast. Dialogue at once ensues, as the Canon and his servant greet the company courteously and express their desire to join them. The Host at once enquires if the Canon will be able to tell a merry tale or two to amuse them all, and the Yeoman assures him that he can. We soon find, however, that the relationship between master and man is far from harmonious, and the canny Host becomes suspicious of the Canon, whose clothes are so poor as to belie the claims made for him by his servant. Seeing this, the Yeoman is encouraged to speak of the alchemical practices in which they are engaged, but he makes no attempt to pretend that alchemy works: 'We blondren evere and pouren in the fir' (670) he states. Though they make people believe that they can change a pound of gold into two, 'yet is it fals' (678). Tension increases as the Canon overhears and tells his Yeoman to be silent, to stop slandering him and revealing their secrets. The Host, however, encourages the Yeoman to disregard the threats, and there is nothing for it but for the Canon to hurry off as rapidly as he had come 'for verray sorwe and shame' (702). The Yeoman then takes advantage of his chance to reveal all.

COMMENTARY: At this point in *The Canterbury Tales* we have a perfect opportunity to appreciate the extent to which Chaucer's genius had developed over the years. *The Legend of St Cecilia*, probably written in about 1373, is stiff, lifeless and colourless compared with the dramatic, subtle and original *Canon's Yeoman's Prologue*, and the tale that follows it. The sudden bursting in of two new pilgrims upon the cavalcade, quiet and thoughtful as it is at that moment, is enlivening and stirs the reader's curiosity. In other collections of tales, one follows another with the minimum of interchange between the tellers, but here it is almost as if the tales are mere interpolations into the real life drama of the journey to Canterbury. We have a keen sense of real people interacting: the Host deeply suspicious of the newly-arrived Canon, yet prepared to trust and encourage his servant, it seems. The Yeoman is at the end of his tether, and ready enough to uncover the dishonest practices of his master, seeing himself safe among the crowd of pilgrims. The Host by this time has weighed up the Canon and dismissed him as unworthy of serious consideration; and the Canon tacitly accepts the situation, knowing he has no leg left to stand on, so he takes himself off. Almost the whole episode, with its nuances of feeling as well as its forthright revelations, is in the form of naturalistic dialogue, its interchanges suggesting, with great psychological realism, the inevitable tensions and conflicts of life itself. These characters speak like individuals and come to life before our eyes, unlike Cecilia and Valerian in the previous tale.

The Canon's Yeoman's Tale

The Yeoman begins the first part by describing his life over the past seven years as the Canon's assistant. He gives a very detailed technical account of the work and then goes on to speak of the way in which people become deeply involved in it, in the hope of discovering the philosophers' stone and turning base metals into gold. It is unpleasant work, and often there are explosions, but still the experiments go on.

In Part 2, the Yeoman tells a story of how a wicked canon who is an alchemist deceives a foolish priest into giving him money in exchange for his secrets. By his trickery, the canon convinces the priest of his ability to make gold and silver out of other metals. Three times over, this canon makes it appear that another metal has turned into precious metal in the heat of the furnace, but he does it by slipping in the precious metal when the priest is not looking. It looks such a simple process that the priest readily gives him forty pounds for the secret, whereupon the canon departs and is never heard of again.

The Yeoman ends with an extended warning against a desire for gain that is ready to work against God's purposes, for it cannot hope to prosper.

COMMENTARY: The first part of this tale indicates Chaucer's extensive though amateur knowledge of the alchemical processes, and his scepticism. It has been said that *The Canterbury Tales* are about work, and of none of the tales is it more true than of this one, in which so many of the technical details of the alchemist's work are mentioned. Chaucer makes poetry out of this complex subject by showing how it affects people's lives. The Yeoman who can contain his disgust no longer, and the dupes of the alchemist who continue their useless experiments in the face of constant failure, provide a human context for the 'text-book' information that takes up many lines of the first part. It is not only of the theory that we are informed, but of the practice to. We see how alchemy affects the health of those who practise it and of the psychological effect it has on those who become involved with it. The bizarre ingredients that the alchemists use are reminiscent of the extraordinary stock-in-trade that the Pardoner carries round with him, and both characters may be said to have similar intentions – cheating people out of their money. The Yeoman reels off a list of the processes involved in alchemy, and much still more recondite lore besides, but he has no illusions about 'This cursed craft' (830), as he calls it. It is a pursuit to which, as with gambling, people become addicted in their lust for gain, led on by false hopes – a bitter-sweet activity which causes them to sacrifice everything for the sake of continuing the crazy search, though it only leaves them stinking of brimstone or sulphur. The search for the 'philosophres stoon' the 'elixer' (862–3) sounds romantic, but the reality is sordid and morally reprehensible. The smell of brimstone suggests the fumes and fires of hell, and leads on to another unpleasant aspect of alchemical practices: the explosions that often occur. A dramatic passage of dialogue conjures up the scene, providing also a visually-realised context for the exposé of this pseudo-scientific experimentation (920–54). The group of men involved try to account for the mishap – some blaming it on the condition of the fire, or the kind of fuel, or on a cracked pot – and then they try to salvage something from the scattered remains. So the first part of the Yeoman's tale ends, with his completely disillusioned account of his recent occupation. It helps to complete Chaucer's picture of the medieval world of work in which rogues and honest men contend for a livelihood, reminding each other from time to time of the spiritual ideals to which all pay lip-service, but which few manage to attain.

The second part of *The Canon's Yeoman's Tale* is quite different from the first, being a *fabliau*-like story of trickery in which, however, money rather than sex is the mainspring of the action. Though the story concerns a priest happily living in London, in the house of a woman who looks after him very well, it is concerned solely with how the foolish man is exploited by the cunning canon. It has been suggested that the tale may have been written for a different audience, the Canons of the King's Chapel at Windsor; and also that Chaucer may once have been cheated by a certain Canon Shuchirch, who was also an alchemist, but nothing is known for certain.

Chaucer shows us another aspect of the world of deception and exploitation in this tale, which we may evaluate in the context that he has already created for us. In *The Franklin's Tale* 'trouthe ... the hyeste thyng that man may kepe' (1479) was the inspiration to noble deeds of self-sacrifice, but, read as a whole, *The Canterbury Tales* suggest that in ordinary life there are few absolutes. 'Trouthe' for the Canon is not the same thing as 'trouthe' for Arveragus in *The Franklin's Tale*. For the Canon it is in no way binding. 'Trouthe is a thyng that I wol evere kepe', he says reassuringly (1044), but his declaration is no more than a useful sentiment to encourage confidence in his victim.

This is a tale about the impostures of alchemists, rather than about individuals. It shows how easy it is to impose on people blinded by their own greed for money, and exactly how the tricks themselves can be carried out. Instead of individualised characters in the story of the alchemist and his victim, however, we are given a firm impression of the personality telling the story. His deeply felt loathing of alchemists and all their tricks comes out strongly: 'Ther is a chanoun ... Amonges us, wolde infecte al a toun' (972–3), and such a man is to be seen as a Judas, a man who would betray his best friend. The service that he offers stinks (1066–7). Chaucer gives us a sense that the Yeoman is keenly aware of his audience and alert to what may be going through their minds: 'This chanon was my lord, ye wolden weene?' (1088). He assures them that this man was not his master – his real master, another canon, was even cleverer and more unscrupulous. We see the Yeoman's sense of his own situation expressed in both moral and physical terms: he is ashamed of his master, and even feels his face burn with embarrassment at being associated with him. We as readers trust him when he makes this declaration, perhaps most of all because the Host has seemed to do so.

The flexibility of Chaucer's mature verse gives us a sense of the speaking voice as the Yeoman tells his story, varied by straightforward narration, rhetorical questions addressed to the pilgrims, and passages of dialogue which come alive with their exclamations and their changing intonations. We hear the wheedling tones of the canon: '"Leene me a mare," quod he, "but dayes three"' (1026), and later his too emphatic assurances '"What!" quod this chanoun, "sholde I be untrewe?"' (1042). The Yeoman is careful to emphasise the slick little touches of courtesy by means of which the deception is helped along, and which show how lamentably unsuspecting the stupid priest is, as for example, 'At youre comandement, sire, trewely' (1063); 'in tokenyng I thee love' (1153); 'Graunt mercy' (1156); 'Goddes blessing, and his moodres also,/ ... have ye, sire chanoun' (1243–4); culminating in the final words of the canon as he departs with his enormous winnings, 'farwel, grant mercy!' (1380).

The grateful politeness of the priest as his deception is systematically carried out adds to the subtle irony of what is in itself a simple tale. It may be more sharply appreciated by comparison with *The Pardoner's Tale*, in which equally evil characters converse with each other in a different context, in dialogue bristling with fearsome oaths. In *The Canon's Yeoman's Tale* we have as it were a real-life illustration of the figure mentioned in the Temple of Mars in *The Knight's Tale*, 'The smylere with the knyf under the cloke' (1999). The canon, however, occasionally allows himself a nicely-feigned exclamation of manly impatience such as 'Thow fynde shalt ther silver, as I hope./ What, devel of helle! Sholde it elles be?' (1237–8). The determined energy of the swindler is communicated through the reiteration of imperatives (1119 ff.) which give a sense of the extent to which he is in command of the situation, while at the same time he appears to be simply inviting the 'sotted priest' in a friendly way to participate in the mysterious processes himself. Take this instrument; send your man away; shut the door; now let me take over; wipe your face; let's sit down and have a drink; get up; go and fetch a stone; look; hurry away now – these are only some of the injunctions which indicate the wicked canon's power over his victim, and which give a dynamic quality to the verse.

Elsewhere, the Yeoman gives us a sense of witnessing the alchemical process itself as he piles up clauses descriptive of what is going on, for example in 'He putte this ounce of coper in the crosselet,/And on the fir . . . /And caste in poudre . . . /And in his werkynge . . .' (1308–11). We gaze fascinated, as it were, not understanding what is going on any better than the priest did, but waiting to see what will happen as we carefully watch the trickster and his victim. These passages, alternating with dialogue, give variety to a rather sombre tale and supply a good example of the art that conceals art, for the tale is so well unified and flows so easily from its beginning to its melancholy conclusion, that – as so often with Chaucer – it is difficult to see just how he makes it work. We have to look very closely indeed to become aware of the nuances of tone and the syntactic patternings that give subtlety to what seems at first sight very straightforward narration.

The Yeoman, when after some general comments he finally ends his tale, provides us with a kind of moral, a 'poynt' (1480), a clearly stated message for audience and reader: it never does to go against the will of God, and so, by implication, against nature. A similar meaning emerges from *The Franklin's Tale*: it is dangerous to upset the ecology, as Dorigen found when she reproached God for surrounding the coast of Brittany with dangerous rocks, and wished that they were not there. But this is not the only meaning that the tale bears, of course: 'Thou shalt not covet' is another theme of equal significance; and finally, it sharply reminds us of the commandment that every *fabliau* exemplifies; 'Thou shalt not be a fool!'

The Manciple's Prologue and Tale

At this point the pilgrims have reached 'a litel toun' called 'Bobbe-up-and-down' (which unfortunately no longer exists as such), and here they have trouble with the Cook, who is drunk, starts to quarrel with the Manciple and then falls off his horse. As usual in the linking passages between the tales, there are lively and dramatic interchanges between the pilgrims, and here the Manciple does not refrain from expressing his disgust at the disgraceful state of his fellow pilgrim, with a very vivid analysis of what the condition implies. The Host eventually succeeds in reconciling Cook and Manciple, and then the latter tells his tale, since it is obvious that the Cook is incapacitated.

The story

Phoebus (the sun-god in Greek mythology) has come to earth in human form. He has a snow-white crow that is able to speak; he also has a wife whom he dearly loves, and of whom he is very jealous, but she has a lover. One day the crow is a witness to the lovers' meeting. When

Phoebus comes home, the crow (in those days crows could sing more sweetly than the nightingale) begins to sing 'Cuckoo! cuckoo!', meaning that by her adultery his wife has made Phoebus a cuckold. Phoebus is not at all grateful for the information, and in anger pulls out the crow's white feathers, turns it black, and leaves it only able to caw instead of singing. Everyone should take note, and refrain from telling other people things that they would rather not know.

COMMENTARY: The tale of the crow is an entertaining fable, but comparison with *The Nun's Priest's Tale* is revealing. The story of the cock and the fox provided Chaucer with a medium for a tale rich in contemporary comment of various kinds, subtle in its use of a wide range of different literary techniques, and superbly witty and amusing parodic effects. The tale of the crow clearly did not suggest to him any such possibilities for enrichment: it is a pleasantly told fable, but no more – though the story itself engages the attention, especially when the officious crow tiresomely insists on revealing all to Phoebus, rubbing in the worthlessness of his wife's lover and the exact details of what went on in the husband's absence.

Talking birds are always appealing, of course, but the crow has nothing to say of comparable interest to Chauntecleer's conversation with his wife Pertelote in *The Nun's Priest's Tale*: it would be too much to ask that Chaucer should perform such a *tour de force* twice.

The Parson's Prologue and Tale

The pilgrims have now almost arrived, and the Host calls on the Parson for the last tale, suggesting another fable. The Parson refuses to tell what he regards as a frivolous kind of tale, but offers something of a moral and virtuous nature, in prose. Everyone agrees that such a tale would be highly appropriate in the circumstances, and the Parson tells his tale, a sermon on Penitence.

It seems probable that Chaucer, now approaching the end of his life, was forced to conclude *The Canterbury Tales* without achieving the much more ambitious aim (four tales for each pilgrim) set forth in the *General Prologue*. The serious note on which the story-telling ends is appropriate to end the fictional pilgrimage to Canterbury, but also the real pilgrimage of life, which was drawing to a close for Chaucer. His thoughts were increasingly directed, it seems, to spiritual matters, for after *The Parson's Tale* follows Chaucer's *Retractation*, in which he says farewell to the reader, rejects his more frivolous works, and hopes for salvation at the last.

The Parson's Tale

The tale – which is a typical medieval sermon rather than a narrative – begins with a discussion of penitence and allied matters such as penance and sin. It moves on to a study, taken from another source, of the Seven Deadly Sins, a topic which seems always to have interested medieval people. In fact, it has much more interest for the modern reader, too, than one might expect. For example, under the heading of pride, the Parson discusses contemporary fashion in considerable detail, condemning the too revealing, tight-fitting clothing of men and the 'outrageous array of wommen' (429), too. Despite these denunciations, however, the sermon is not entirely negative in its content, for it balances its criticism with some definitions of the positive qualities such as 'gentilesse', that may be substituted for foolish pride in trivial things. The section on anger is equally comprehensive, for this sin leads to swearing, superstition, lying, flattery and other sins that proceed from wicked words. The analysis of each sin is followed by a passage suggesting remedies for it, usually very schematic and containing carefully enumerated points for easier remembering. When the sins have all been dealt with, the Parson returns to the discussion of penitence, ending with a definition of the fruit of penance: it is 'the endless blisse of hevene' (1076), where the body, that before was 'syk, freele, and fieble, and mortal, is inmortal, and so strong and so hool that ther may no thyng apeyren it' (1078) and where hunger, thirst and cold are replaced by joy in the knowledge of God. The passage reminds us of the hardships and sufferings of life which many of Chaucer's contemporaries had to undergo, and of how they necessarily looked to a world of lasting happiness beyond this one. From our reading of *The Canterbury Tales* we can see how they snatched such pleasures as life afforded with eager hands, but always with the fear of judgment and a haunting anxiety about the means of salvation.

Chaucer's 'Retracciouns'

At the very end of *The Canterbury Tales*, following *The Parson's Tale*, we find the words 'Heere taketh the makere of this book his leve', a passage which has come to be known from what follows, as Chaucer's 'Retracciouns' or Retractation. Chaucer had reached the end of his life, and knew that he would never complete the great scheme of *The Canterbury Tales*; contemplating death, he asks the reader to pray for him and to pray that his sins may be forgiven. He expresses anxiety about his 'enditynges of worldly vanitees', and lists a number of his poems which he considers as tending towards sin. The list includes some of his greatest works, but by the strictest standards of medieval religion,

Chaucer believed that they had to be rejected, for they had not been written primarily and solely to the glory of God. In asking forgiveness for these writings, he gives thanks for the work that he has done that cannot be considered as morally reprehensible or trivial, mentioning his translation of Boethius' *Consolation of Philosophy*, and 'othere bookes of legendes of seintes, and omelies, and moralitee, and evocioun' (1087). Not all of the works of which he speaks in these two categories have survived, however.

In this sad farewell, we have Chaucer's most personal utterance and message to his readers, and at the same time an indication of the underlying seriousness of his mind, whatever may have been the impression created by many of his more light-hearted works. At the end of his life, he is doing what he had recommended his young audience to do at the conclusion of *Troilus and Criseyde*, turning 'hom fro worldly vanyte', turning his heart to God, and looking upon this world as 'but a faire . . . that passeth soone as floures faire' (V.1837–41).

Chaucer's short poems

Chaucer must have written many short poems that have not survived. The most interesting of those that have – less than twenty in number – divide themselves into three main groups. There are, first of all, the philosophical, Boethian poems, 'The Former Age', 'Fortune', 'Truth', 'Gentilesse' and 'Lak of Stedfastnesse' which may well express Chaucer's own attitude to life more directly than any other of his poems. There are some courtly, amusing little love poems, 'To Rosemounde' and 'Merciles Beaute', and there are some humorous poems which include 'Chaucers Wordes unto Adam, His Own Scriveyn', the 'Envoys' to Scogan and to Bukton, and 'The Complaint of Chaucer to his Purse'. The other short minor poems believed to be by Chaucer are of much less interest, and will not be discussed here.

In 'Truth,' Chaucer writes of this complex virtue, 'the hyeste thyng that man may kepe' (*The Franklin's Tale*, 1479), that he had upheld throughout his work. 'Truth' in the medieval sense stands for personal integrity, for loyalty to others, and to an ideal. It is one of the attributes of God, and in a philosophical sense means 'reality'. In this poem Chaucer urges his reader to turn away from worldly vanities, by an effort of will, so that he may find peace in the eternal unchanging spiritual reality. Chaucer advocates acceptance ('receyve in buxumnesse', or obedience), and emphasises that this world is alien to us, for we are only pilgrims passing through it. He recognises in this poem the reluctance of our partially animal natures to engage in high spiritual endeavour, apparently addressing this short poem of stern encouragement to his friend, Sir Philip Vache. (Vache (1346–1408), who held an official position at court, is thought to have fallen from favour in the late 1380s.) The unwilling 'beast' of the third stanza links ingeniously with the name of Vache (meaning 'cow' in French) in the last stanza.

In 'Fortune', a more complex poem divided into three parts, Chaucer defies Fortune to distress him, for the faculty of reason enables him to gain mastery over himself and his emotions. He asserts that he only suffers in so far as he permits himself to be miserable. Fortune answers him by saying that whether good or ill, what she sends is still under God's control; only heaven can give respite from the constant changes of earthly life. Again, men are like the beasts in their ignorance; but only in this world can they be subject to Fortune's changes.

In 'The Former Age' and 'Gentilesse', Chaucer turns to other Boethian ideas. In the first, he speaks of the Golden Age, before sin came into the world, when man was uncorrupted by greed and envy and treachery. 'Gentilesse' takes up the argument put forward in *The Wife of Bath's Tale*, that 'gentilesse' (noble behaviour) is not a virtue that can be inherited, but comes from God, and does not derive from noble birth.

'Lak of Stedfastnesse' offers advice, in its last stanza, to King Richard II. It laments the state of the world, and urges the King to cherish his subjects and restore stability to the realm by upholding justice, truth and honour. It was advice of which, tactfully though it was offered, Richard unfortunately did not avail himself.

In much lighter vein we have a *ballade*, 'To Rosemounde', a poem in which Chaucer mocks the extravagances of conventional courtly love-lyrics. Rosamond's jewel-like beauties have a striking effect upon her admirer, and the mere sight of her dancing is ointment to the wound that she has inflicted. Because she shows him so little favour, he sheds tears by the barrel; and he is deeper in love than a fish that is served up at table is deep in jelly. The elegant, closely rhymed stanzas make the absurd images that denote the lover's plight more amusing in their incongruity.

'Merciles Beaute', a triple *roundel*, is, like the previous poem, an example of a fashionable French verse-form. It is a complex and sophisticated poem of courtly compliment. The lover desperately wounded by his lady's beautiful eyes, is at the point of death, for she will show him no pity. Since she will not love him, he gives up, and ends by exulting in his escape with his life from love's prison. Like 'To Rosamounde', the poem plays with and makes fun of love conventions; it is not meant to describe a real situation.

The poems in the last group are also humorous, though in 'Chaucers Wordes unto Adam, His Owne Scriveyn', the author's complaint of the mistakes made by the scribe employed to copy his poems conveys, in seven lines, a sense of deep exasperation. 'The Complaint of Chaucer to His Purse', with its graceful puns, also evokes the reader's sympathy. His purse is his 'lady dere', and he naturally grieves that she has become a light lady. Chaucer then turns from the language of love to religious imagery: his purse is his saviour, and he is 'shaved as close as any friar'. He ends with an address to the King, in the hope that help may be forthcoming from him.

There are also two poems addressed to younger friends: 'Lenvoy de Chaucer a Scogan' and 'Lenvoy de Chaucer a Bukton'. In the first, he reproaches Scogan for offending the god of love by giving up his pursuit of a lady who would show him no favour. Chaucer fears that the god's displeasure may be extended to include him too. Despite the humour, there is a note of melancholy: Chaucer's muse, he says, is rusting in its sheath and he fears that his work will be forgotten with the passing of time. He feels, too, that he is 'in the wilderness', out of favour at court, and asks Scogan to see that he is not permanently neglected, by putting in a good word for him.

To Bukton, Chaucer solemnly gives a little warning against falling into the trap of marriage, urging him to read the 'Wyf of Bathe' on the subject before committing himself.

Part 3

Studying Chaucer

Literary forms and conventions

Chaucer used a wide range of different genres and verse-forms in his works. At the beginning of his career he was strongly influenced by French poetry, and we see in some of his surviving short poems examples of such popular French forms as the *rondel* and the *ballade*. They are formal, stylised, often highly patterned courtly lyrics. In *The Book of the Duchess*, he made extensive use of French models, borrowing material and adopting a similar verse-form, that of the octosyllabic rhyming couplet.

The French love-vision or dream-poem was also fashionable when Chaucer was writing. He had himself translated the most famous of such poems, the *Roman de la Rose*; and we see him writing in this genre himself in *The Book of the Duchess*, *The House of Fame*, *The Parliament of Fowls* and *The Legend of Good Women*. It allowed him to transport the reader out of the everyday world into one in which adventures of the mind could take place, enabling him to communicate matters that could less easily be presented in a more direct, matter-of-fact way.

In *Troilus and Criseyde*, Chaucer abandoned the form of the dream-poem and took as setting for his story of love and tragic loss, the 'real' world of courtly life. In the poem, he made use of the high style appropriate to serious themes, as can be seen from the invocation to mythological figures, and from the formal songs. Towards the end of the poem, he expressed the hope that the work might take its place, even if only a lowly one, with the greatest works of literature by the great classical writers. In it, Chaucer also achieved a great variety of effects, dramatic and colloquial, comic and lyrical, as well as solemn.

The Canterbury Tales include examples of many more different genres or kinds of writing. *The Knight's Tale* is a fine example of romance, which, like *Troilus and Criseyde*, is serious and has tragic elements. In it we can see examples of the high style in such set pieces as the descriptions of the temples, of the lists, and of Arcite's funeral, which lend it appropriate dignity. Many of the conventional features of romance can also be seen in it, such as the idealised characters, the theme of love, and the supernatural element, but it has a philosophical depth not to be found in all romances.

The Miller's Tale and *The Reeve's Tale*, on the other hand, are examples of *fabliaux*, stories very popular in medieval France, in which women often get the better of jealous husbands, and lusty young clerks or students display their intelligence and manly prowess. In these stories, realistic contemporary settings offset amazing (and amusing) plots, and contrast with the courtly and idealised settings of romance.

Elsewhere we see the form of the saint's life, also very popular in the Middle Ages, in *The Tale of St Cecilia*, and *The Prioress's Tale*; the *exemplum* in *The Pardoner's Tale* of the three revellers; and the sermon in the Parson's prose tale. As in *The Pardoner's Prologue*, so in *The Wife of Bath's Prologue*, we have the form of the confession, earlier examples of which can be found in the *Roman de la Rose*. In *The Franklin's Tale* Chaucer gives us an example of the Breton lay, and in *Sir Thopas* he burlesques the tail-rhyme romances which provided contemporary entertainment but were often of little literary value.

The Nun's Priest's Tale is a beast-fable, while in *The Monk's Tale* Chaucer gives us a generous sample of medieval tragedy, in the string of stories of those who fell from the height of good fortune to disaster and death. In *The Tale of Melibee* he tells a moral tale in prose, instead of verse – a story dull to most modern readers, but apparently far more pleasing to some of his contemporaries than the amusing *Sir Thopas*. His greatness as a poet is shown in the range of different forms with which he experimented, as well as in what he accomplished in them.

Chaucer had much respect for the great writers of the past, from whose work he often drew the raw material for his own poems and whose forms he adapted for his own use. Earlier versions of the stories which Chaucer tells in *The Canterbury Tales* can be seen in Bryan and Dempster's *Sources and Analogues of the Canterbury Tales* (see Bibliography). Not only are the old stories given new life by Chaucer, but they are often enhanced by the presence of the poet in his own work as storyteller. This was a conventional device in an age when poems and stories were as frequently read aloud to an audience by the author, as intended for private consumption, but Chaucer often presents himself in his own work as a rather comic character. Sophisticated, experienced man of the world though he must have been, in *The Canterbury Tales* he assumes the guise of a naive, easily impressed fellow pilgrim, reporting on his companions. By contrast, in the passages which link the tales together, in which Chaucer describes the reactions of the pilgrims to the story they have just heard and introduces the teller of the one that is to follow, the lively dialogue and dramatic interchanges between the pilgrims are strikingly original, and all the more so in an age when it was customary to use traditional material as the basis for narrative.

These linking passages give a vivid and realistic picture of some aspects of the pilgrimage – for example, of the antagonisms and rivalries between some members of the company. In the *General Prologue* to *The Canterbury Tales* we have what seems to be a remarkably realistic portrayal of the pilgrims, yet each one remains a representative figure. Chaucer often builds up a comprehensive impression of the life-style of his characters through the very realistic detail in which he describes them, and which he incorporates into their tales. This can give an impression of the daily preoccupations and even the patterns of thought of his characters – for example, the homely everyday world of the Wife of Bath and even her cast of mind are revealed as she speaks her Prologue. Chaucer makes sparing use of metaphor and symbol; when he does – as in *The Franklin's Tale* when the garden and the rocks are laden with symbolic meaning – the effect is all the more impressive.

Chaucer is a master of the *double-entendre*, and his constant use of irony contributes significantly to the subtlety of his writing. Irony implies saying one thing and meaning another, creating a tension between what at first sight appears to be the meaning, and what the author really wishes his readers to understand. When, for example, Chaucer tells us of the Summoner that 'A bettre felawe sholde men noght fynde' (648) or of the Pardoner that 'He was in chirche a noble ecclesiaste' (708) we discern that there may be two views about these characters. Only a naive reader could take the statements literally; and yet while we know that we cannot accept their literal truth ourselves, we suspect that these comments represent what the two characters actually think of themselves.

Verse forms

In earlier poems, such as *The Book of the Duchess*, Chaucer used octosyllabic couplets, with four stresses in each line, a rather constricting form which he later abandoned for the longer line with five stresses. When Chaucer discovered and adopted the longer line – in effect, the iambic pentameter – it allowed him a far greater flexibility, for he did not keep rigidly to the rhythmic pattern. He kept to the pattern of five stresses, but by sometimes omitting the first unstressed syllable of a line, or by adding extra unstressed syllables, he was able to adapt his verse to the needs of dialogue, and make it very free-flowing. Chaucer's stanzaic verse is also based on the line with five stresses, but with a different rhyme scheme, as for example in *Troilus and Criseyde*. Here he used rhyme royal (rhyming *ababbcc*). Just as, when he wrote in couplets, the lines are often run on so as to create larger units of meaning (instead of being end-stopped), so sometimes when he wrote in stanzaic form, Chaucer carried on the sentence from one stanza to the next, creating a complex unit of meaning.

Chaucer's use of rhetoric

Though we now tend to despise rhetoric as implying vapid, laboured writing, it was not so regarded in the fourteenth century, when it was a regular part of the educational curriculum. It was one of the Seven Liberal Arts on which medieval education was based, and valued as the art of persuasive speaking and writing. Though Chaucer sometimes gently mocks rhetoric in *The Canterbury Tales*, his writing nevertheless depends for its effect upon his skilful use of its techniques. In much of his work he uses rhetoric with an art that conceals art.

There were many books that taught the subject in the Middle Ages, most of them deriving from earlier Latin works by such classical writers as Cicero and Horace. One of the most famous of medieval treatises was the *Nova Poetria* of Geoffrey de Vinsauf, written about 1200, long recognised as an authoritative work on poetry. Chaucer refers to Geoffrey (Gaufred) in *The Nun's Priest's Tale* (3347). The art of rhetoric was considered to have five main branches. These included *invention* which enabled the writer to find a novel way of expressing what he had to say. Most medieval writers took material which was already well-known as their subject matter, often retelling stories which had long been familiar in such a way as to give them new meanings. *Invention* helped them to do this successfully, rather than to create new stories as one might have expected. *Disposition* was another branch of the subject, concerned with the way in which narrative threads were to be interwoven to make a complex story, while *Elocution* related to the actual choice of vocabulary and syntax, which naturally had to be appropriate to the purpose and the style of the composition.

The rhetoricians devised a very detailed and elaborate system for effective writing. The device of *diversio* or digression might be used to add interest, as we see in *The Wife of Bath's Tale* when she interpolates the story of Midas, presumably to the increased pleasure of her medieval audience. There were a variety of approved ways of amplifying the basic material, but the effect was not necessarily to pad it out; rather, as often with Chaucer, the amplification enabled the audience to come to a deeper understanding of significance and subtleties. Rhetorical devices were intended to enhance meaning and intensify poetic effects, by such means as repetition and onomatopoeia and the skilful use of description and illustration. Of course they could become boring if used clumsily; though the modern reader's impatience with rhetorical devices may derive more from a change in taste over the centuries than from a lack of skill on the part of the author. We do not react with much enthusiasm to the excellent example of *occupatio* in *The Knight's Tale* (2919–66) in which the Knight says that he is *not* going to tell us about Arcite's funeral, and then does so at great length. Medieval man loved lists, and we do not. We may regard the stylised description of Blanche in *The*

Book of the Duchess (948–60) as tiresomely artificial because we are unable to appreciate the convention with which it accords, but the portrait of Alison in *The Miller's Tale*, which seems so much more lifelike, depends even more on the craftsmanship with which Chaucer has selected and presented significant detail. The simple enumeration of the lovely features of Blanche has given way to a more complex and advanced technique.

The modern reader does not need to be able to pick out and comment on the various rhetorical devices, or the technical terms by which they are known, in Chaucer's writing, but he does need to be aware of the artistry and subtlety of effect which characterises Chaucer's poetic achievement and helps to make his work memorable.

Chaucer's language

After the Norman Conquest of Britain in 1066, the language of the upper classes in England became Norman-French. It was the language of government and of culture, though learned works were usually written in Latin. By the fourteenth century, however, French was dying out, and Chaucer's first language was of course English, though since he was attached to the court, he had a fluent command of French.

Chaucer's English was the English of the south-east, the dialect of the area around London, which eventually became predominant and which developed, in the course of time, into modern standard English. As a result, Chaucer's poems are easier to understand now than those of his contemporaries. Such poems as *Piers Plowman* by William Langland, which appeared in three versions between 1362 and 1392, and *Sir Gawain and the Green Knight* by an unknown author, were written in more northern parts of England and the dialect in which they were composed is hard to read today. A very large proportion of the words used by Chaucer are still in the language today, though the spelling may not be familiar, and sometimes the meaning has changed in the course of time. Many of the words that go to make up Chaucer's large vocabulary were in origin French or Latin words which were being absorbed into English at this period, in a process which both enriched and extended the range of the language.

The pronunciation of Chaucer's English

Vowels
A clear distinction was made between short and long vowels.

Short vowels
a   between modern 'cut' and 'cat'
e   as in modern 'bed'

i   as in modern 'sit'
o   as in modern 'top'
u   as in modern 'put' (not as in 'cut')

In such words as 'companye', 'love', 'come(n)', 'konne', 'sonne', 'moche' and 'yong', the letter *o* was written instead of *u*, and should be pronounced as *u*.

Long vowels

a   as in modern 'car', 'father'
e, ee   (open – that is, where the equivalent modern word is spelt with *ea*) as in modern 'where'
e, ee, ie (close – that is, where the equivalent modern word is spelt with *ee* or *e*) as in modern 'fate'
i, y   as in modern 'machine'
o, oo   (close – usually found in words whose vowels in modern equivalents are pronounced like 'blood', or 'food' or 'other') pronounced as in modern 'so'
o, oo   (open – should be used for those words in Chaucer where the modern equivalent vowel is sounded like 'throat', 'most') pronounced as in modern 'law', 'saw'
u   as in modern 'pew', or French 'tu'

Diphthongs

ai, ay,
ei, ey   between modern 'day' and 'die'
au, aw   as in modern 'out', 'bounce'
eu, ew   as in modern 'new'
ou, ow   as in modern 'boot', if the vowel in the equivalent modern word is sounded like 'house' or 'through'
ou, ow,   as in modern 'grow', if the vowel in the equivalent modern
ough   word is sounded like 'grow' or like 'thought'

Final –e

Many words ending in *–e* in Chaucer's poems require the *–e* to be pronounced, because it is essential to the rhythm of the line. Before a silent vowel or a silent *h*, the final *–e* is not pronounced.

Consonants

Most consonants are like their modern English equivalents. Exceptions are:

gg   either hard as in modern 'dagger', or soft as in modern 'bridge'
gh   as in German 'ich'
gn   both consonants should be pronounced at the beginning of a word; the *g* is silent when the combination appears in the middle of a word
kn   both consonants should be pronounced

l   pronounced before *f, v, k, m*
wr both consonants should be pronounced

Grammar

Nouns

In the plural and possessive, nouns add *–es* if they end in a consonant, *–s* if they end in a vowel.

Some nouns are unchanged in the genitive singular; for example, *his lady grace* (his lady's favour).

Some make their plural with *–n*; for example, *ye, yen* (eyes); *hosen* (stockings).

Pronouns

ich is used as well as 'I' for the 1st person.

his is used for 'its' in the 3rd person singular, genitive.

you and *ye* are the polite forms of the 2nd person.

thou and *thee* are the familiar forms.

The distinction between polite and familiar forms was still recognised in Chaucer's time.

In the 3rd person plural, Chaucer uses *hem* for 'them' and *hir* for 'their'.

Adjectives

If they are monosyllables ending in a consonant, a final *–e* is added in the plural, as also on those occasions in the singular when they precede the noun they qualify, and when they follow 'the', 'this', 'that', 'my', 'your' and other possessives, and a noun in the genitive case.

Adverbs

Many adverbs end in *–ly*, as in Modern English, while others end in *–liche*. A few end in *–e*; for example, *loude* (loudly).

Verbs

The Infinitive often ends in *–en*.

The Present Tense: the 3rd person singular ends in *–eth*. The plural often ends in *–en*; for example, 'Thanne longen folk to goon on pilgrimages'. The Imperative often ends in *–eth* the plural form, which is used as a sign of politeness to a single person.

The Past Participle is often prefixed by *y–*; for example, 'by aventure yfalle'.

Hints for study

Modern readers sometimes find it hard to appreciate Chaucer to the full because they read his poems with the wrong expectations. It is helpful to remember that with Chaucer's poems as with myths and folk tales, Bible stories and fairy tales, legends and fables, the story comes first, not the characters. From the stories deeper meanings often emerge, meanings true for human nature in general. They are not so much stories about particular individuals, but about how human beings behave. Thus we are not given individual character studies as in modern fiction, though Chaucer's characters sometimes seem remarkably life-like. In *The Knight's Tale*, for example, the two young lovers, Palamon and Arcite, are almost indistinguishable, as the story requires them to be, for here Chaucer is concerned not with their individual psychology, but with, among other things, the apparent arbitrariness of life and the difficulty of coming to terms with it.

The characters, therefore, are often representative figures: the type of the young lover, or of the beautiful girl, or of the jealous husband. If they are not fully individualised or motivated and do not seem to develop, it is because the story does not require it, and partly also because medieval writers looked at human beings in more general, representative terms.

We should look beneath the surface level of the stories for the deeper meanings, as Chaucer explores the experience of falling in love, of enduring suffering, of hating and lusting, envying and succumbing to flattery – always as the observer of human nature. He does not write about himself and his own feelings, though he accompanies us as guide and storyteller through the poems.

For some people, the language of Chaucer constitutes a difficulty. This can often easily be overcome by listening to a reading of the poem in the original pronunciation, on tape or record, while following the text. Reading the poem aloud to oneself, as correctly as possible, helps understanding too, and familiarises the reader with the text. The general sense of a passage will often be revealed, and individual words can be looked up afterwards if necessary.

Confusion can arise from those words that have changed their meaning since Chaucer's day, while remaining in the language. Words such as 'gentil' and 'sely', which look like 'gentle' and 'silly' but mean 'noble' and 'innocent', are examples. Negative forms can be puzzling too: the reader needs to be on the alert for verbal forms made negative by the addition of 'ne', as in 'nil' – (will not), and 'noot' (combining 'ne' and 'not', to mean 'not know').

Chaucer does not really need to be read in translation, indeed translations are best avoided. But where translation is required of the student, he should try to put the text into good modern, literal prose, keeping as close to the original as possible.

Some background knowledge is vital for an understanding of religious and 'scientific' references (for example, to astrology and alchemy), and wider reading is very worthwhile, whether of Chaucer himself, to fill in the historical background of the fourteenth century, or by making use of modern critical studies. Many of the concepts that play an important part in Chaucer's work (such as 'trouthe', patience and obedience) can only be understood in the context of medieval life and thought.

The first essential is, of course, to gain a good working knowledge of the text itself, then to understand the implications of what Chaucer is saying so as to come to a deeper understanding of the story. The more literary aspects of the poem also require attention – for example the structure and the style – for an understanding of the way in which Chaucer tells his story. What kind of story is it? And to what *genre* does it belong? How does Chaucer present characters and setting? How does he use classical and biblical allusions? How functional are digressions from the main subject? What use does he make of rhetoric – of symbolism – of proverbial sayings? Such questions may help to lead the reader to a fuller awareness of the art that conceals art, by means of which Chaucer's work makes its appeal.

Part 4

Bibliography

Texts

ROBINSON, F. N. (ED.): *The Works of Geoffrey Chaucer*, 2nd edn, Oxford University Press, London, 1957. The standard text, to which reference is made throughout this Handbook.

DONALDSON, E. T. (ED.): *Chaucer's Poetry: An Anthology for the Modern Reader*, Ronald, New York, 1958. Contains both text and excellent discussion of the poems.

BAUGH, A. C. (ED.): *Chaucer's Major Poetry*. Appleton-Century-Crofts, New York, 1963. Very well glossed.

CAWLEY, A. C. (ED.): *The Canterbury Tales*, Everyman, Dent, London, 1958. Well glossed.

Sources

BRYAN, W. F. AND DEMPSTER, G. (EDS.): *Sources and Analogues of Chaucer's Canterbury Tales*, Routledge and Kegan Paul, London, 1958.

GORDON, R. K. (ED. AND TRANS.): *The Story of Troilus*, Dent, London, 1964. Translations of earlier versions of the story, with Chaucer's text and Henryson's *Testament of Cresseid*.

Background Studies

BOASE, ROGER: *The Origin and Meaning of Courtly Love: A Critical Study of European Scholarship*, Manchester University Press, Manchester, 1977.

BREWER, D. S.: *Chaucer in His Time*, Longman, London, 1973.

BREWER, D. S.: *Chaucer and His World*, Eyre Methuen, London, 1978.

BREWER, D. S.: *Writers and their Background: Geoffrey Chaucer*, Bell, London, 1974.

CURTIUS, E. R. (TRANS.) AND TRASK W. R.: *European Literature and the Latin Middle Ages*, Routledge and Kegan Paul, London, 1953.

DU BOULAY, F. R. H.: *An Age of Ambition: English Society in the Late Middle Ages*, Nelson, London, 1970.

EVANS, JOAN (ED.): *The Flowering of the Middle Ages*, Thames and Hudson, London, 1966.

LEWIS, C. S.: *The Discarded Image: An Introduction to Medieval Literature*, Cambridge University Press, Cambridge, 1967.

LOWES, JOHN L.: *Geoffrey Chaucer*, Oxford University Press, London, 1962. The first chapter contains an introduction to Chaucer's astronomy.

MATHEW, GERVASE: *The Court of Richard II*, John Murray, London, 1968.

NEWMAN, F. X. (ED.): *The Meaning of Courtly Love*, New York State University, Binghampton: Centre for Medieval and Early Renaissance Studies, Annual Conference March 1967, Proceedings, New York, 1968.

PANTIN, W. A.: *The English Church in the Fourteenth Century*, University of Toronto Press, Toronto, 1955.

ROBERTSON, D. W. (JR.): *Chaucer's London*, John Wiley, New York and London, 1968.

STEVENS, JOHN E.: *Music and Poetry in the Early Tudor Court*, Cambridge University Press, Cambridge, 1961. Has an especially interesting chapter on 'The Game of Love'.

General and Critical Studies

BOLTON, W. F. (ED.): *The Middle Ages, Sphere History of Literature in the English Language*, Vol. I, Sphere Books, London, 1970. Contains four useful essays on Chaucer.

BOWDEN, MURIEL: *A Reader's Guide to Geoffrey Chaucer*, Thames and Hudson, London, 1964.

BOWDEN, MURIEL: *A Commentary on the General Prologue to the Canterbury Tales*, Macmillan, London, 1948.

BREWER, D. S.: *Chaucer*, 3rd edn, Longman, London, 1973.

BREWER, D. S. (ED.): *Chaucer and Chaucerians, Critical Studies in Middle English Literature*, Nelson, London, 1973.

BURROW, JOHN: *Ricardian Poetry, Chaucer, Gower, Langland and the Gawain Poet*, Routledge and Kegan Paul, London, 1971.

BURROW, JOHN: *Medieval Writers and their Work: Middle English Literature and its Background, 1100–1500*, Oxford University Press, London, 1982.

CAWLEY, A. C. (ED.): *Chaucer's Mind and Art*, Oliver and Boyd, Edinburgh and London, 1969.

CURRY, WALTER C.: *Chaucer and the Medieval Sciences*, 2nd edn, Allen and Unwin, New York and London, 1960.

DONALDSON, E. T.: *Speaking of Chaucer*, Athlone Press, London, 1970.

EVERETT, D. AND KEAN P. M.(EDS.): *Essays on Middle English Literature*, Clarendon Press, Oxford, 1955.

HOWARD, D. R.: *The Idea of the Canterbury Tales*, University of California Press, Berkeley, 1976.

HUSSEY, M., SPEARING, A. AND WINNY, J.: *An Introduction to Chaucer*, Cambridge University Press, Cambridge, 1965.

HUSSEY, S. S.: *Chaucer: An Introduction*, Methuen, London, 1971.

JORDAN, R. M.: *Chaucer and the Shape of Creation*, Harvard University Press and Oxford University Press, New York and London, 1967.

KEAN, P. M.: *Chaucer and the Making of English Poetry*, 2 vols., Routledge and Kegan Paul, London, 1972.

LAWLOR, JOHN: *Chaucer*, Hutchinson, London, 1968.

MANN, JILL: *Chaucer and Medieval Estates Satire*, Cambridge University Press, Cambridge, 1973.

MEECH, S. B.: *Design in Chaucer's Troilus*, Greenwood, New York, 1959.

MUSCATINE, CHARLES: *Chaucer and the French Tradition*, University of California Press, Berkeley and Los Angeles, 1957.

MUSCATINE, CHARLES: *Poetry and Crisis in the Age of Chaucer*, University of Notre Dame Press, Indiana, 1972.

NEWSTEAD, HELAINE: *Chaucer and His Contemporaries: Essays on Medieval Literature and Thought*, Fawcett, New York, 1968.

PAYNE, R. O.: *The Key of Remembrance*, Greenwood, New York, 1963.

ROWLAND, BERYL: *Companion to Chaucer Studies*, Oxford University Press, New York and London, 1968.

RUGGIERS, P. G.: *The Art of the Canterbury Tales*, University of Wisconsin, 1965.

SCHOECK, R. J. AND TAYLOR, J. (EDS.): *Chaucer Criticism: The Canterbury Tales* (Vol. I) and *Troilus and Criseyde and the Minor Poems* (Vol. II) University of Notre Dame, Indiana, 1960.

SPEARING, A. C.: *Criticism and Medieval Poetry*, Arnold, London, reprinted 1972. Contains some essays on Chaucer.

SPEARING, A. C.: *Medieval Dream Poetry*, Cambridge University Press, Cambridge, 1976.

SPEARING, A. C.: *Chaucer: Troilus and Criseyde*, Arnold, London, 1976.

TATLOCK, J. S. P.: *The Mind and Art of Chaucer*, Gordian, New York, reprinted 1966.

WAGENKNECHT, E. C.: *Modern Essays in Criticism*, Oxford University Press, London, 1959.

WHITTOCK, TREVOR: *A Reading of the Canterbury Tales*, Cambridge University Press, Cambridge, 1969.

General reference books

CROSS, F. L.: *Oxford Dictionary of the Christian Church*, Oxford University Press, London, 1957. An invaluable source of information about many aspects of medieval religion.

RADICE, BETTY: *Who's Who in the Ancient World*, Penguin Books, Harmondsworth, 1971. Very helpful for mythological references.

Records and tapes

There are a number of excellent recordings of readings of Chaucer's poetry in the original Middle English pronunciation in the series *The English Poets, Chaucer to Yeats.* They are produced by the Argo Record Company, 115 Fulham Road, London S.W.3, in association with the British Council. Argo also produce a record, *Medieval English Lyrics*, which includes 'Angelus ad Virginem', mentioned in *The Miller's Tale.*

Index

Further titles

AN INTRODUCTORY GUIDE TO ENGLISH LITERATURE
MARTIN STEPHEN

This Handbook is the response to the demand for a book which could present, in a single volume, a basic core of information which can be generally regarded as essential for students of English literature. It has been specially tailored to meet the needs of students starting a course in English literature: it introduces the basic tools of the trade – genres, themes, literary terms – and offers guidance in the approach to study, essay writing, and practical criticism and appreciation. The author also gives a brief account of the history of English literature so that the study of set books can be seen in the wider landscape of the subject as a whole.

Martin Stephen is Second Master of Sedbergh School.

STUDYING SHAKESPEARE
MARTIN STEPHEN AND PHILIP FRANKS

Similar in aims to *Studying Chaucer*, this Handbook presents an account of Shakespeare's life and work in general, followed by a brief analysis of each of the plays by Shakespeare which might usefully be studied as background reading for a set book. Philip Franks then throws a different light on the study of Shakespeare by giving an account of his experiences of Shakespeare in performance from his perspective as a professional actor and member of the Royal Shakespeare Company.

Martin Stephen is Second Master at Sedbergh School; Philip Franks is a professional actor.

A DICTIONARY OF LITERARY TERMS
MARTIN GRAY

Over one thousand literary terms are dealt with in this Handbook, with definitions, explanations and examples. Entries range from general topics (comedy, epic, metre, romanticism) to more specific terms (acrostic, enjambment, malapropism, onomatopoeia) and specialist technical language (catalexis, deconstruction, *haiku*, paeon). In other words, this single, concise volume should meet the needs of anyone searching for clarification of terms found in the study of literature.

Martin Gray is Lecturer in English at the University of Stirling.

THE ENGLISH NOVEL
IAN MILLIGAN

This Handbook offers a study of the nature, developments and potential of one of the central features of English literature. It deals with the English novel from the historical, thematic and technical points of view, and discusses the various purposes of authors and the manner in which they achieve their effects, as well as the role of the reader. The aim is to bring to light the variety of options at the novelist's disposal and to enhance the reader's critical and interpretive skills – and pleasure.

Ian Milligan is Lecturer in English at the University of Stirling.

ENGLISH POETRY
CLIVE T. PROBYN

The first aim of this Handbook is to describe and explain the technical aspects of poetry – all those daunting features in poetry's armoury from metre, form and theme to the iamb, caesura, ictus and heptameter. The second aim is to show how these features have earned their place in the making of poetry and the way in which different eras have applied fresh techniques to achieve the effect desired. Thus the effectiveness of poetic expression is shown to be closely linked to the appropriateness of the technique employed, and in this way the author hopes the reader will gain not only a better understanding of the value of poetic technique, but also a better 'feel' for poetry as a whole.

Clive T. Probyn is Professor of English at Monash University, Victoria, Australia.

ENGLISH USAGE
COLIN G. HEY

The correct and precise use of English is one of the keys to success in examinations. 'Compared with' or 'compared to'? 'Imply' or 'infer'? 'Principal' or 'principle'? Such questions may be traditional areas of doubt in daily conversation, but examiners do not take such a lenient view. The author deals with many of these tricky problems individually, but also shows that confidence in writing correct English comes with an understanding of how the English language has evolved, and of the logic behind grammatical structure, spelling and punctuation. The Handbook concludes with some samples of English prose which demonstrate the effectiveness and appeal of good English usage.

Colin G. Hey is a former Inspector of Schools in Birmingham and Chief Inspector of English with the Sudanese Ministry of Education.

The first 200 titles

The author of this Handbook

ELISABETH BREWER graduated from the University of Birmingham, and taught English in several Birmingham secondary schools. In 1956 she went to the International Christian University, Tokyo, for two years with her husband and family. While in Japan she taught English language in Hitotsubashi University, and lectured in English literature at Tokyo Women's Christian College. In 1965 she moved to Cambridge, and since then has lectured in English literature at Homerton College of Education, now an Approved Society of the University of Cambridge. Her publications include *From Cuchulainn to Gawain: sources and analogues of Sir Gawain and the Green Knight* (1975), translated from Old French. She has edited, with her husband D. S. Brewer, an abridged version of *Troilus and Criseyde* (1969). She is also the author of York Notes on *Troilus and Criseyde* and *The Miller's Tale*.